Love That Will Not Let Me Go

Modern American Literature
New Approaches

Yoshinobu Hakutani
General Editor

Vol. 19

PETER LANG
New York • Washington, D.C./Baltimore • Boston
Bern • Frankfurt am Main • Berlin • Vienna • Paris

Marguerite Tjader

Love That Will Not Let Me Go

My Time with Theodore Dreiser

Edited by
Lawrence E. Hussman

PETER LANG
New York • Washington, D.C./Baltimore • Boston
Bern • Frankfurt am Main • Berlin • Vienna • Paris

Library of Congress Cataloging-in-Publication Data

Love that will not let me go: my time
with Theodore Dreiser / Marguerite Tjader and Lawrence E. Hussman, ed.
p. cm. — (Modern American literature: new approaches; 19)
1. Dreiser, Theodore, 1871–1945—Relations with women. 2. Novelists, American—20th century—Biography. 3. Tjader, Marguerite—Relations with men.
I. Tjader, Marguerite. II. Hussman, Lawrence E. III. Series: Modern American literature (New York, N.Y.); vol. 19.
PS3507.R55Z6654 813'.52—dc21 [B] 97-51355
ISBN 0-8204-4034-5
ISSN 1078-0521

Die Deutsche Bibliothek-CIP-Einheitsaufnahme

Love that will not let me go: my time with Theodore Dreiser / Marguerite Tjader and Lawrence E. Hussman, ed. –New York; Washington, D.C./Baltimore; Boston; Bern; Frankfurt am Main; Berlin; Vienna; Paris: Lang.
(Modern American literature; Vol. 19)
ISBN 0-8204-4034-5

Cover design by James F. Brisson.

Front cover photo of Marguerite Tjader by Consuelo Kanaga;
courtesy of Hilary Harris.

Contents

Photographs

Editor's Foreword

Marguerite Tjader is remembered today primarily by specialists in American literary history. Most of these specialists, moreover, grant her career importance only through its connection with Theodore Dreiser. Tjader worked intermittently for Dreiser during one of the most fascinating and controversial, if still one of the least understood, stages of the novelist's life. The two first met in 1928 when his fame as the author of the best-selling masterpiece *An American Tragedy* was at its highest. She became his literary typist and amanuensis for several subsequent periods during the years when he lost his newly acquired financial security in the stock-market crash; reevaluated his previous opposition to communism; became a vocal advocate for victims of social injustices including, among others, striking Kentucky coal miners and Spanish Civil War refugees; and moved through the study of biology at East Coast laboratories (Woods Hole and Cold Spring Harbor) toward affirmation of a benevolent Creative Force. In 1944 Tjader joined Dreiser at his request in Los Angeles, where he was revising his perennial novel in progress, *The Bulwark*. She helped him see that climactic work through to its completion in the late summer of 1945, a few months before his death.

But Marguerite Tjader was herself a fascinating person of some literary distinction. She published an artistically successful, though now forgotten novel, *Borealis,* in 1930. In the latter part of the thirties and early forties, she established and edited a significant left-wing magazine, *Direction*. In 1965 her *Theodore Dreiser: A New Dimension* provided firsthand testimony about the novelist's spiritual sea change at the end of his life. In 1974 she edited, with John McAleer, Dreiser's massive collection of philosophical essays and miscellaneous observations called *Notes on Life*. She also wrote two books on religious subjects, *Mother Elisabeth* (1972) and

Birgitta of Sweden (1980). At the time of her death on April 7, 1986, at the age of eighty-four, she was working on a history of the Mexican branch of the Sisters of St. Birgitta. Her unfinished literary projects also included two novels in manuscript, an incomplete study of the architect Le Corbusier, and a memoir about her relationship with Dreiser, the latter of which is introduced through this foreword.

Ms. Tjader was born in New York City on November 24, 1901, the daughter of Richard and Margaret Tjader, who were wealthy but eccentric evangelists. Richard Tjader, whose family traced its roots to a Swedish soldier at the time of the Protestant Reformation, had established a reputation in Stockholm as a flamboyant preacher in the Free Church movement by the time he came to the United States on November 11, 1898. In New York, he met and married Margaret Thorne. The Thornes had made a fortune in New York goods distribution, banking, and finance. An index of the Thorne family's importance can be gauged by the guest list at Margaret's coming-out party. It included Grover Cleveland, railroad magnate James J. Hill, and Oscar Wilde. By the time Margaret, at age thirty-five, met widowed Richard Tjader, however, she had given her life to her own evangelizing work. After the couple's marriage, they joined proselytizing forces and founded the Church of the Strangers in New York City. Their own material fortune grew thanks to Richard's talents as an inventor, notably of the "Tjader Interdeck-Davitt," a device for lowering lifeboats from between the decks of ships.

Richard Tjader's flamboyance continued unabated throughout the rest of his life. In 1906, for example, he led an expedition to East Africa for the American Museum of Natural History and returned to New York laden with trophies, including then-unknown species of waterbuck and bushbuck subsequently named after him. He later accompanied Teddy Roosevelt on African safaris and in 1910 published *The Big Game of Africa*.

When Richard Tjader died in 1916, he was survived by his wife and three of his six children. Of the four children born during his previous marriage in Sweden, three had been drowned with their mother in a boating accident. Marguerite, who, along with her brother Dickie, had been born in New York City, was sixteen at the time of her father's death. During the next few years she pursued her education at private schools and then studied art at Bryn Mawr College and Columbia University, a curriculum that prepared the way for her writing and editing career. With the appearance of *Borealis* in 1930, that career was off to a promising beginning. During the middle thirties while she was writing and translating in

France and Switzerland, she became active in the international peace movement. In 1937 she founded the important liberal magazine *Direction* and between that year and 1945 served as its editor. *Direction*'s list of contributors included Dreiser, John Dos Passos, Erskine Caldwell, Richard Wright, and many other leading writers of her generation.

The tragedy at Hiroshima sealed Tjader's commitment to pacifism. In the early thirties she became a convert to Roman Catholicism. She then deeded her extensive, inherited family property in Connecticut to the Swedish Sisters of St. Birgitta while she lived in a carriage house on the grounds and continued to write. Her religious work intensified in the eighties when she made two trips around the world with stops in the Soviet Union to contact Russian Orthodox Church leaders concerning the Catholic ecumenical movement.

Tjader completed the memoir that fills most of the following pages in the mid-1970s. Approximately ten years had elapsed since the publication of her first Dreiser book, and fresh material and new perspectives on the novelist's life had since come to the reading public's attention, including the controversial W. A. Swanberg biography. Tjader's belief that Swanberg's and some of the other books published after hers did not reveal genuine understanding of the man she knew prompted her to write about him again. In a note to me dated October 5, 1976, she followed up on an earlier conversation about her intentions, with more specifics: "I have some wonderful letters which Dreiser wrote to me and which I had hoped to incorporate into another book about him. As I think I have told you, this would be a book about his philosophy of love, ending with the *greater love,* which was his love for God the Creator." [Tjader's emphasis]

Tjader's memoir faithfully follows the course outlined in her note. It should, therefore, receive welcome from specialists looking for an added perspective on the last seventeen years of Dreiser's life. It should also prove provocative to the increasing numbers of female scholars who have an express curiosity about Dreiser as well as the naturalistic movement in American literature, to those who study women's memoir as a genre, and especially to the feminists and others interested in the evolving psychology of twentieth-century women as they have struggled toward liberation.

For those seeking information about Dreiser the writer and the man, Tjader's remembrances include observations about his creative methods as well as a number of important personal revelations. Among the latter, perhaps the most striking is Tjader's description of Dreiser's sensitive approach to loving and lovemaking as opposed to the legend of unadorned lechery. That legend has persisted and contributions to it keep accumulating. In 1995, for example, Yvette Eastman added new revelations to the fund with her somewhat disturbing personal account of her relationship with the novelist, *Dearest Wilding* (University of Pennsylvania Press). Tjader's attempt to erase the historically disseminated caricature of Dreiser as a thoroughgoing sexist represents a long overdue first step toward a rehabilitation of his personal reputation. Here too is testimony to the physical relationship between Dreiser and Tjader, so long the unspoken suspicion of scholars. Tjader's confirmation of the emotionally and physically successful sexual melding experienced with him provides as well a rejoinder to his psychologist niece Vera Dreiser's hypotheses. In her book *My Uncle Theodore* (Plainview, N. Y.: Nash Publishing, 1976), Vera argued that Dreiser's many love affairs were characterized by impotent sexual encounters throughout an unavailing "lifetime struggle for a meaningful love relationship," a situation that supposedly resulted from a perpetual "state of arrested development." Emphatically not so on any count, Marguerite's version of events argues. And there are other nuggets in her memoir. It describes in some detail Helen Dreiser's strained feelings toward her at the time of the novelist's death. Just what was going on between the two women in those last days of Dreiser's life has long been the subject of interest among his biographers. Facts presented about Dreiser's friendships with John Cowper Powys and Allan Hunter also add to the record.

But perhaps the best reason to ponder Tjader's pages has to do with the interrelationship between Dreiser's life and his art. In a literary age during which the reader's demand for psychological truth in the packaging of fictional characters has been strongest, Dreiser, even more than most other modern novelists, relied on introspection to animate his. Those characters, from Carrie Meeber through Clyde Griffiths to Etta and Solon Barnes in *The Bulwark,* dramatize the desires their maker struggled ceaselessly to fulfill in his own life. But it is most notably Eugene Witla in *The 'Genius'* and Frank Cowperwood in the financial trilogy that demonstrate conclusively Dreiser's concurrence in Schopenhauer's assertion that sexual fulfillment constitutes the hidden agenda behind all human striving. In Dreiser's novels money, power, fame, social acceptance, and even art, serve as means to the end of connection with the right sexual partner (or partners). Any new evidence of how Dreiser actually conducted his relationships with women, and especially so important a one as that with Marguerite Tjader, could prove most helpful.

Contemporary feminists may, however, find the Marguerite Tjader who emerges from her memoir at least initially perplexing. In the vocabulary of today's women's movement, her unabashed adulation of Dreiser and her sometimes overly involved rationalizations of his unquestionably hurtful promiscuity may evidence seriously addictive and codependent behavior. How could this woman, who displayed such independence of thought and action in most other precincts of her life, virtually genuflect in memory of such a man? Whatever his literary achievements, he littered lovers in amazing numbers. And, after all, Tjader had been a published novelist, a successful editor, a seasoned world traveler, one of the few woman mountain climbers in her day to conquer the Matterhorn, a volitional divorcee at a time when broken marriages were the rare exceptions, and a free spirit who took her own sexual pleasure with less than socially approved discretion. Her unapologetic affair with Dreiser, including the married Dreiser, was clearly not her only unsanctioned relationship, for example. For those readers who cannot understand what would motivate such a largely liberated woman to so revere someone like Dreiser, her attitude toward him will seem, on the surface, constructed, impossible to credit.

But Tjader's memoir can also be seen in the context of its time and valued as an index of the limitations on liberation for women then. She was, after all, in her mid-seventies when she began the project and not about to abandon the point of view that had evolved during her relationship with Dreiser and which was subsequently reaffirmed in her 1965 book about him. Despite the fact that the postmodern feminist movement had gained considerable momentum by the 1970s, Tjader was not particularly attentive to its achievements, and no hints of the historic changes taking place around her make their way into her memoir. On the other hand, her reminiscences are frequently colored by rhapsodic celebrations of Dreiser's own seemingly measureless independence and consequent prerogatives. These evocations of his empowering freedom may be properly glossed as, at least in part, the product of envy, the latent lament of a talented woman living in a day when a woman's worth was still measured by the man to whom she was linked as much or more than by her own accomplishments. (And a healthier response than the jealousy unconsciously displayed by the many male critics who express disgust over Dreiser's sex life). Moreover, "unaccountable" dependency on men was not unknown among the earlier female proponents of liberation or among those whose public lives seemed fully liberated. One thinks in these connections of Simone de Beauvoir's willingness to endure continuing psychological abuse in order to continue her relationship with Jean-Paul Sartre or Marlene Dietrich's need for a nonstop parade of male lovers, for example. And even the contemporary feminist Naomi Wolf has admitted to "abject" submission to the dictates of infatuation. Were Dreiser not an internationally known figure commanding scholarly curiosity, Tjader's memoir would still be valuable as a psychography of an emancipated woman of her time.

At any rate, Tjader's mental makeup as revealed in her reminiscences invites conjecture. To some, she may seem a victim of her parental tapes, replaying her mother's dependency. Margaret Tjader had also been a strong woman capable of independent thought even bordering on the bizarre, but she too had gravitated to a dominant man in a man's world. It was Richard Tjader, after all, who made the trips to Africa in search of souls and record game kills while his wife stayed in the States with the children. Was Marguerite driven to Dreiser as a learned behavior? Or was she in fact so liberated herself that she saw him as an ideal sexual partner who demanded as little commitment as she was willing to give? And, of course, human nature's complexity being undisputed, might she not have at least in part been attracted to him by the desire to collect a trophy lover, in some sense making her bid for a fraction of what she believed would be his literary immortality? Such questions serve the useful function of reminding us that we dare not judge the admittedly limited liberation of yesterday's women too harshly by the standards of today.

Having had the advantage of knowing Marguerite Tjader as I did, I have no doubt that she loved Dreiser inordinately, whatever the baser motives or fated responses that might have, to a greater or lesser degree, accounted for her continuing attraction to him. She told me often during our friendship about his talent for connecting psychologically with women, to perform as what she describes in her memoir as a "doctor of souls." For most critics and his major biographers, Dreiser's hypersexuality makes it difficult to accept the idea that he could successfully interact intellectually and spiritually with what he regarded as a physically attractive woman. After all, most of the novelist's own writings concentrate on the primacy of sexuality in relationships almost to the exclusion of other considerations. Take particularly in this context his sketch "Emanuela" in *A Gallery of Women*. In it he muses over a female acquaintance's insistence on a platonic friendship with him despite her beauty and he attributes her incomprehensible refusals of his advances to her being "either undersexed or too purely mental, or something." But Dreiser's seemingly total inability to conceive of an intellectual association with Emanuela and his many other outrageously sexist stands throughout his works may have had more to do with male posturing than actual practice. Certainly in her memoir, Tjader tries to locate the center of his appeal in his willingness to listen rather than his bedroom technique, the former virtue linking him to an unlikely counterpart, Woody Allen, whose film persona movie critic Molly Haskell once called a "Casanova of conversational empathy." Tjader believed that Dreiser's womanizing had to be judged in relationship to these ameliorating traits. Her estimate of him, in fact, meshes with one of his descriptions of Lester Kane in Jennie Gerhardt. In a passage that could double as a Dreiser self-justification, the novelist pleaded for a sympathetic understanding of his protagonist's appropriation of Jennie:

> Although on the face of things he appeared to be a hunter and destroyer of undefended virtue, he was yet a man of such a complicated and interesting turn of mind that those who are inclined to be radically intolerant of his personality had best suspend judgment until some further light can be thrown upon it. Not every mind is to be calculated by the weight of a single folly, not every personality judged by a single passion

For too long Dreiser's relationships with women have been dismissed as passionate follies.

Gender analysts and general readers, both male and female, will have to decide whether Tjader's unmistakable lack of distance from her subject, despite the passage of so many years and her avowed purpose of stressing the best in Dreiser, have resulted in a recognizable portrait. Her intense love for him obviously never diminished. That will doubtlessly be for some an impediment to their acceptance of her perspective, just as her several ardent defenses of him at academic meetings disconcerted many of the assembled scholars unused to such strong feeling, and cast her as a somewhat controversial figure.

The core of Marguerite Tjader's message in this memoir is that Dreiser's great talent for loving, and not just loving women but also male friends and in a more abstract way the poor and the oppressed, was the salient feature of his personality. As she sees it, that love and compassion animated his whole approach to life. In the process of urging such a view of Dreiser, she points up how the novelist's compassion for and understanding of humanity melded with his irresistible attraction to the world's "ineffably gorgeous" texture, leading logically toward his affirmation of a Creative Force. In this context, even his addiction to female beauty becomes perfectly logical. One has only to remember the epiphany achieved by Frank Cowperwood's mistress Berenice Fleming, sparked by a Hindu guru, near the close of Dreiser's last novel, *The Stoic*. Intent after the death of her lover on understanding his lifelong pursuit of dazzling women, Berenice travels to India to study with the mystic. When asked about Cowperwood's predilection, the guru responds that the financier was worshipping "the face of Brahman reflected through all forms and designs," not simply the individual women he desired sexually:

> When you see a man being drawn to a beautiful face, do you think that it is a handful of arranged molecules that really attracts him? Not at all! Behind those material particles there must be and is the play of divine influence and divine love. The ignorant man does not know it, but yet, consciously or unconsciously, he is attracted by it, and it alone.

The temptation here, of course, is to chalk such an explanation up to Dreiser's "Hollywood Hinduism," to see it as a rationalization of the kind that Warren Beatty might embrace. But there have been few if any attempts at explaining sexual desire that have been more notably persuasive. Seen in the burnished glow of his last years and the novelist's emotional acceptance of a benevolent Creative Force, not only the women Dreiser needed but also what many might regard as his lustful pursuit of them could be given this positive spin. And knowing Marguerite Tjader as I did, I'm sure he must have had her, no doubt among others, in mind when he crafted the guru's speech.

Editing Tjader's manuscript involved cutting away certain quotations from Dreiser's *Notes on Life* as well as some other material that did not substantially enhance the record as established by Dreiser's biographers. In 1976 when she began her memoir, Tjader was fresh from editing, with John McAleer, *Notes on Life* for the University of Alabama Press. She had undertaken that project as a labor of love. Having been faced with space limitations and the necessity of rejecting some of the notes she thought important, she hoped to propagate them in her memoir. But in the manuscript she left in my care at the time of her death, the stream of her remembrances was clogged with too many interruptions from the notes. I also found it advisable to omit short sections concerning the novelist's friendships with Charles Fort, Ralph Fabre, and George Douglas, as well as a few passages devoted to a recapitulation of Dreiser's early years in Indiana. On the other hand, I allowed to stand some material that Tjader previously treated in her *Theodore Dreiser: A New Dimension*—a few passages because incidents are explored more fully here and others because they supply an explanatory environment for her narrative. Just as Tjader was sensitive to Dreiser's unique way of framing his ideas and regretted the tampering done by his editors, so I have been careful to preserve her distinctively interpunctuated style. I have included in an appendix the original introduction to the memoir as written by Tjader to provide an indication of the editorial process. I have also appended the contributions made by both Dreiser and Tjader to *Direction*.

I wish to express my heartfelt thanks to those who helped me accomplish my work. In particular, I thank Marguerite Tjader's son, Hilary Harris, for granting permission to pursue the project and to include his mother's letters and photographs. The University of Pennsylvania Library, through its Theodore Dreiser Papers, Special Collections, also permitted quotation of some of the novelist's letters, excerpts from unpublished parts of *Notes on Life,* and contributions to *Direction*. Nancy M. Shawcross, Curator of Manuscripts, helped smooth this process. Elizabeth Mossman and Lee Ann Draud at the University of Pennsylvania Library also assisted by supplying copies of letters. Harry Ransom Research Center, The University of Texas at Austin, graciously granted permission to publish some of the letters Tjader sold to that institution. Cathy Henderson there was most helpful in easing access to these letters. Finally, I wish to thank Evelyn Belcher and Jane Baker for their preparation of the edited manuscript.

LAWRENCE E. HUSSMAN

Marguerite Tjader. Photo courtesy of Hilary Harris.

Author's Introduction

Theodore Dreiser was a figure baffling to many in his own generation. His image was often distorted by critics, frequently lesser personalities who neither understood him nor his way of writing and thinking. Even to many of his friends who acknowledged his greatness, he was an enigma. But as I look back on my long relationship with him, certain of his qualities persist in my memory, and grow clearer in perspective.

There has been much discussion about Dreiser's attitudes toward sex, which were once considered scandalous. Even today, he is sometimes remembered as much for his many affairs as for his books. Yet no one has tried to understand how his personal philosophy of love colored his relationships with women as well as those with his male friends.

Because of his extraordinary frankness in discussing his own emotions and his ability to describe his characters' feelings, Dreiser offers a special opportunity to study the psychology of male sexuality as he so well understood and practiced it. In his related philosophy of love for all persons, there are no pornographic details but only a sublime poetry of the senses, a mystique, and a great longing for continuity, something beyond the deep human agonies and joys in which he fully participated.

The term "bioenergy" might be used today to define and study a certain subtle but sometimes measurable force that can be emitted from the vitality of a person, affecting others as love, hate, healing power, or causing telepathy, attraction. Dreiser did not know the word, but such a force was real to him, coming from person to person, or perhaps streaming through the universe, to be picked up by sensitive souls. Dreiser used the word "love" in this sense. It encompassed, beyond the love of the sexes and for close friends, a concern for the handicapped, for prisoners, for human rights victims, for sufferers from poverty, crime, violence, or despair. For Dreiser, the lack of love, like the lack of food for the starving, explained much of man's misery.

We should not forget, however, that love of work, above all, was his central drive. Ever diligent, he forced himself to the task at hand, no matter how tired he felt, discouraged or depressed. "I go out so little," he wrote to me once, "heaven for me should consist of a desk and a window and a chair afloat in space." But because beyond his work he was himself exceptional—the psychoneurotic, the artist, the mystic, the sensualist, the wildly passionate saint or devil, all of these categories might apply to him, though none fit him exactly—he interested the public as a man.

Who is going to signal his essential characteristics as the number of those who knew him grows ever smaller? Since I was privileged to have worked with him during several different periods, I feel compelled to add to and correct the record, as a contemporary witness. Since his work belongs to the future, so does his stature as a man. I want to share my experience of knowing him and many of his friends, and to speak about the way he loved persons and life. These reminiscences and certain unpublished letters, material from his published work and his files, as well as some of my photographs make up this manuscript. I hope these will enhance understanding of this unique man, Dreiser, and his fascinating philosophy of love.

MARGUERITE TJADER

Love That Will Not Let Me Go: My Time with Theodore Dreiser

by Marguerite Tjader

> The pride of the peacock is the glory of God.
> The lust of the goat is the bounty of God.
> The wrath of the lion is the wisdom of God.
> The nakedness of woman is the work of God.
> —from William Blake's *Proverbs of Hell*

Dreiser liked to quote these lines, especially the second. He felt akin to Blake, in his lusty, daring way of putting words together in concepts near blasphemy, yet with a respect and love for Biblical language, which haunted both writers.

The strict moral code of the turn-of-the-century Catholic church, in which he was raised, left Dreiser in his youth with no hope of fulfilling the desires that were arising or surging in his blood. Awkward and fearful though he was in his teens, he reached out for girls, and found to his surprise that they responded. From then on, the lust of the goat gripped him. In describing a character, he once wrote:

> For just now he was intensely concerned mentally with thoughts of girls. . . . In fact, he was cursed with an overwhelming hunger for physical sex gratification. The curve of a cheek or neck, the grace of movement, the glance in the eyes or the touch of a hand of any attractive girl moved him with a kind of energy that was electric in its character.

Dreiser was writing here of young Stewart Barnes in *The Bulwark*. As I worked with him on this Quaker novel in the months just before his death, he told me that the character of Stewart quite closely resembled his own at the adolescent stage, and his description of the fictional boy's response to girls continued:

> He was roused, brightened, made to thrill at the mere sight of them. And, true to his nature, he was not definitely interested in one, but in all. Seldom did he walk down the street that he did not see a girl who was disturbingly attractive to him. He yearned after her, not realizing how fickle was his mood.[1]

Here, Dreiser sets the tone of his own varietism; there would be no end to the passages we might quote from his novels and his autobiographical writings on these subjects. But I wish to present only new material here. Nor is it necessary to dwell on earlier emotions; the fires of lust burned in Dreiser all his life, sometimes uncontrolled, sometimes tempered. They were an inseparable part of his creative force; they gave him that energy, and perhaps what is called animal magnetism, behind the fascination of his mind and his conversation. Meeting him at a social gathering, at the height of his career, one could immediately feel the heat of his personal fire, and in his seventies that fire still burned bright, like Blake's tiger "in the forests of the night."

There was nothing cheap or vulgar about Dreiser's approach to sex. He loved women with something almost like reverence. Even the great sensuality that aroused itself in all his nerves was, in a way, purified by its vigor. Not a mental sensuality, deliberate or calculating, or debasing to his partner, but a generous adoration of the body, the deep love of woman, perhaps a love of many women, all women, but for the moment fully expressed as the love of one, the one in his arms, with whom he could share the delight of the senses, which he raised to a high degree of elegance and importance. There was never an artist, never a lover who had a stronger sense of beauty than Dreiser, a greater need for it, as part of his creation of the living moment. This was essential to his over-emotional, over-sensitive nature. Cold-blooded vices, perversions, or sadistic tendencies were absolutely alien to him. He always sought some loveliness, some illusion of love.

Because I have alluded to Blake's lust of the goat, it should not be assumed that Dreiser was some kind of sex fiend who did not balance this dominant interest with a wide appetite for all the riches of the tumultuous world opening up to him. Strongly moved by nature and all radiance, he had been thrown into a life of poverty in Chicago, after the breakup of his home, and had to take a series of drab, demeaning jobs with little time for dreaming or reading. But once he had the leisure he devoured each mind-shaking book he read, like the novels of Balzac in the libraries of Pittsburgh while he was working on *The Dispatch*. He developed from reporter and newspaper man to writer of short stories and novels. At almost every point, it would seem that destiny had sent him some guide, or inspiring friend. John Maxwell, Joseph McCullagh, his own brother Paul.[2] Then when he came to New York, his contacts multiplied. His world had truly expanded. Yet always against a background of defeats and frustrations, as well as small successes.

Parallel to these milestones of his literary career were emotional frustrations and triumphs; loves and romances. In his youth, his emotions were so strong that he obeyed them without thought of marriage. His first serious relationship showed him something about himself and a girl named Alice, which he reveals in one of his autobiographies:

> I saw myself a stormy petrel hanging over the yellowish-black waves of life and never really resting anywhere. I could not; my mind would not let me. I saw too much, felt too much, knew too much. What was I, what any one, but a small bit of seaweed on an endless sea, flotsam, jetsam, being moved hither and thither by what subterranean tides?

So already, he was detaching himself from the usual pitfalls of romance. Alice loved him, and would have gladly switched to him, though she was engaged to another. But he was not looking for ties, although he had needed her badly at the time. He writes this sentimental tribute to her, which shows the tender heart he carried throughout his life, in spite of his irrepressible philanderings:

> O, Alice, dead or living, eternally sleeping or eternally waking, listen to these few true words! You were beautiful to me. My heart was hungry. I wanted youth, I wanted beauty, I wanted sweetness, I wanted a tender smile, wide eyes, loveliness—all these you had and gave.
>
> Peace to you! I do not ask as much for myself.[3]

Yet later, after other short encounters, Dreiser really fell in love with a charming, intelligent young woman named Sara White from a small town near St. Louis.[4] This was a very different story. She fanned his desires with her own professed love, yet would not yield to his embrace. He loved her enough to consider marriage but had neither money nor position to offer. She was willing to wait, believing in his ability. He pursued his career, seeing her when he could. He visited her home, the old wooden house, under huge trees, the atmosphere of rural America.

Dreiser, the sentimentalist, and also the realist, wrote a poignant description of this interlude with the woman who was to become his first wife in *A Book About Myself*.[5] His sketch intimates what eventually went wrong with his noble experiment in matrimony. Each new day, the turmoil of his newspaper work, his first encounter with New York, both thrilling and bitterly difficult, lessened his delicate love for Jug, his midwestern sweetheart. It was eight years before he was established in New York and able to send for her.

It was already too late. Dreiser now felt only "duty." But it is important to realize that he was once a subdued and hopeful husband. His destiny dictated, he might say, that marriage could not be successful for him. But he did not deliberately avoid it. In fact, he paid a heavy, emotional price for his mistake, as did Jug. After several separations, their final parting came only in 1914. (She died in 1942.) She did not want to give him a divorce, nor did he insist on one. They had had no children, but keeping an official tie made him feel free to pursue others, without the risk of making another marital mistake.

He sought love with many women, always hoping to find the ideal companion, the kindred spirit, the illusion of sexual and temperamental union. But he hardly expected to find it. And when exciting women came along, like Kirah Markham or Helen Richardson, he could enjoy their love without the burden of domesticity or vows of lasting allegiance.[6] Dreiser might have gone down in history as a kind of American Casanova had he chosen to portray his own experiences with women, to the exclusion of other subjects. But frankly, though he often wrote about sexual dramas of his own or of his characters, he was never bogged down, mired, or stuck in his own sensuality. Much as he had suffered in early years from desires, unrequited or rejected, he did not succumb to despair but was able to make literature out of his own failures. And, even later, he could regard his successes with a certain impersonal emotion, if not detachment. The thirst and love of sex was an emotion in itself, never fully satisfied, but always leading on.

As for my story, it attempts only to place Dreiser from the time I knew him, from 1928 on, as a personality, a writer, and a connoisseur of life. I wish to summon up his presence. I hope that he will seem real to readers of the present and future, rather than another complex figure emerging from one more intellectual study.

When I met Dreiser for the first time, at a small dinner party, I knew nothing about him as a writer. His presence simply overwhelmed me; he was a tall man, tremendously alive, with eyes that glowered down on me, full of curiosity and challenge. His head was roundish and sculptured, with a straight nose under heavy brows. Only his mouth was irregular, mobile, and his voice was very deep and hushed, as it were, by some kind of suppressed emotion. Yet he was very much at home here, in this company of close literary friends.

He asked me questions about myself, then turned to his hostess, a charming, large woman who seemed like an opera singer or an actress; warm, emotional, well poised. She was Laetitia, one of the artistic MacDonald family, her brother Dwight MacDonald, the writer, her sister, Maria Jolas, singer and editor of the magazine *Transition*. Our host was Laetitia's husband, Wallace Irwin, the writer.[7]

Laetitia had many talents of her own, especially that of conversation. Indeed, words flew back and forth with great ease, for my handsome southern husband had been a friend of Laetitia's in Louisville.[8] Helen, glamorous and dark-haired, destined years later to become Dreiser's second wife, and who was with him that evening, obviously appealed to him as well. Before the end of the evening, we were all good friends. Dreiser had said that he liked my straight, red hair, braided around my head, and he teased me because I had no job. He said I should do some work for him, and I found myself promising to see him the next day. Helen had also invited us all to come to their next studio party.

At this time of his greatest success, after the publication of *An American Tragedy,* Dreiser lived in the duplex studio which many have described. It was at West Fifty-seventh Street, near Carnegie Hall.[9] Some have said that it was Helen who wished to have this place, worthy of her charms as a hostess, but certainly Dreiser enjoyed it thoroughly himself. For two winters they kept open house on Thursday evenings. They had a fascinating circle of friends; artists, literary people of all sorts, musicians, actors and actresses—many beautiful women.

Here I first observed Dreiser in the full power of his personality, surrounded by many types of fascinating people. Yet he was somehow aloof, inscrutable; engaging in animated, gleeful dialogue one moment, and then moving away, retreating, though he never left the room. Once in a while his glance struck me—troubled me. Why? Perhaps destiny, for our relationship was fated to endure, but at the time, he was merely a thunderbolt out of the blue, a striking presence that could electrify, and go as quickly as a light turned off.

Seeing him here, magnetizing others who were also feeling this current, responding, laughing in the animated atmosphere of the moment, confirmed the challenge I had immediately felt upon meeting him. Here was a free spirit, a wild horse, a great artist of living who understood everything, but would never be tamed to ordinary ways of life. He also had in him great silences and pain. He could speak thunderously to some, mumble a few words to others, to me, all the time keeping some secret behind his penetrating gaze. Yet, I could respond to this spirit and still keep my own integrity. I was young, but already married and restless—I longed for a freedom as great as his, almost more than for love.

I did some work for Dreiser that justified our meeting a few times. It did not matter how often we were able to be alone. He understood all the pros and cons of my marriage and yet did not want the responsibility of giving me advice. He encouraged me to write and work. He seemed to "believe in me," whatever that meant. Or was he just seeing in me the reflection of his own life-force? Often, I had felt discouraged and inwardly very lonely, in spite of the outwardly glamorous life I led.

My marriage was an escape from the early tragedy of losing a beloved father, and then a love affair with a married Frenchman whose life was the sea.[10] So I had brooded, read many books, and was always filled with a great hunger for something else. Someone else, who could not exist, for me. Finally, I had grown tired of my own sense of tragedy. My taste for life was getting stronger. By chance, a handsome bachelor, fourteen years older than I was, fell in love with me and persuaded me to marry. He was a brilliant young lawyer, come up from the South, determined to make a success, professionally and socially, in New York. Serving in the Navy, he had been in France during the last months of the First World War, loved French women and wines, and continued his conquests in the fast-moving city of the twenties. He was delightful and sophisticated, but also subject to fits of depression and anger.

After about two years, when the first storms of emotion were over, he quite frankly sought other women, and instead of being jealous, I also embarked on a series of romantic encounters. He had wanted to teach me the social life, how to dress, how to drink and entertain, and now we were both playing dangerously. Because of my Swedish background, I seemed drawn to foreign types, a White Russian, European musicians. Sometimes my husband accused me of being a bohemian and not as successful as I should be at the social game. But somehow, my heart was not in it, and I felt increasingly alone in the crowd. No one seemed compelling, and often when I drank, instead of feeling buoyed, I felt horribly trapped; afraid of my husband's jealousy, yet not knowing anyone else who came near to being the phantom-lover I longed to find. Then Dreiser came along, and the loneliness was suddenly over. Such people did exist; warm, understanding, tremendous temperaments who could sweep you off your feet, and up into a world where you could breathe a new air of freedom and creation. A lover who seemed also to be a force, disembodied, akin to all artists and writers, who could project the very essence of life.

There was often a third element in our conversation, the personality of some writer whom we both loved, and who illustrated for us the deepest reaches of life. It had begun with John Cowper Powys, whom I tried to describe to Dreiser when he called on me for the first time. I sensed that Dreiser and Powys were two personalities of somewhat the same kind. Feeling strangely challenged, I reached for a slim volume of Powys's poetry called *Samphire,* which had just come out, and said to Dreiser: "Here is someone I would rather know than anyone in the world. You probably never heard of him." Dreiser then uttered the word "Jack" in such a tone that I could sense his affection even before he began to tell me about their deep friendship.[11]

Another temperament who affected us both was Oscar Wilde. When in England for the first time, Dreiser had visited the grim prison where Wilde wrote his "Ballad of Reading Gaol." He also loved *De Profundis* with its aching, religious overtones: The figure of the Christ, the feet of clay, the weary, human face—and Wilde's advice to cure the soul through the senses, and the senses through the soul.

As no subterfuge was necessary, no exaggeration of a personal or possessive love, we felt free to discuss all our emotional involvements and also realized that there was little time for a further exploration of our own relationship. And now he suddenly went off to Arizona, motoring over the desert, sleeping beside his car at night, under the starry heavens. This gave him a sense of wonder and unity with nature, at intervals essential to him.

To fill a gap in the story of my early relationship with Dreiser, some observations can be made about his general attitudes toward love and the emotions. He had always felt that man is governed not so much by his mind as by his instincts, both animal and psychic, or physical and spiritual. Often it is impossible to draw a line between the two, he thought, and easier to classify cerebral motivations and actions.

Many critics have judged Dreiser according to mental standards alone, without realizing that his strength—or what they may consider his weakness—lay in the very fact that he acted on his most basic, sincere, and intuitive feelings and did not try to compete with intellectual writers or thinkers whose knowledge was greater but "drier" than his own. (By drier, I mean unpolluted by those emotions that are stronger than reason or logic.) So he has often been called a confused thinker, inconsistent, maddening to many clear-minded scholars who have never had to wallow in the swamps of emotional conflicts and psychological agonies that lay in Dreiser's world as they did in those of Powys and of Dostoyevsky and of Blake. Anyone attempting to understand Dreiser must take into account his own belief that the heart is more essential to man's life than his brain. His emotions drive him, teach him, and yield the richest fruits of joy, as of despair.

All these emotions, Dreiser felt, grow out of the wellspring of Nature. Sex in all its seriousness, love—perhaps the greatest gift of the gods. Dreiser felt a deep affinity for D. H. Lawrence on the level of the senses. In an unpublished portion of the *Notes on Life,* Dreiser quotes Lawrence on how the blood hates being known by the mind and, on the other hand, the mind and the spiritual consciousness hate the dark blood acts.[12]

Under this quotation Dreiser added a comment about how, at times, a person feels driven by desire, ungoverned by mind. While editing the *Notes on Life,* I found, on a scrap of tracing paper, this very short, handwritten epigram, which stands alone, like a cry: "Lacking the aid of the flesh, the spirit must remain forever ignorant of the highest, the profoundest, the intensest forms of love."

In a mood less anguished, Dreiser commented on the universality of the sex urge. From a long *Note,* unpublished, he examines the different forms it may take:

> All men and women have sex desires in some degree. People of great ability and mental capacity probably have more difficulty in becoming satisfied sexually than people of lesser sensitivity, just as they have more difficulty in being satisfied or adjusted in other phases of their lives. They want, relatively speaking, perfection. And the same force in them, if it does not find realization in the ordinary way, may lead to all kinds of perversions, homosexuality, promiscuity, etc.

> If on the other hand, this force does not achieve equilibrium through an obvious sexual route, it may even be sublimated and take form from frustration in increased activity, mentally, spiritually in creative work in art, government, or what you will. Sex in them may take several forms simultaneously and intermittently. For example, you might have a man of great ability, highly sexed who would take normal paths for sexual realization but who, though partly satisfied, would divert the remaining capacity in some form of frustration, which as energy seeking to spend itself, would influence his work and life in other ways not specifically sexual.
>
> The life of ascetics is an example of this latter form of force. It can scarcely be doubted that ascetic zeal is a form of sublimated sex energy.

Another unpublished note redirects the discussion to the universal wish to be sexually attractive:

> All persons have in some degree the wish to be desired sexually even if they themselves do not desire specifically. This is especially obvious among young people where sex is strongest and freshest, and among the highly sexed of all ages. This sexual exhibitionism is responsible for consciously developed charm, attractiveness of person, etc. It may, also, through a kind of frustration, where satisfaction is not immediately or possibly attainable, cause exhibition in all other phases of life. For example, an unattractive girl or boy may turn their sexual exhibitionism into intellectual channels, or to sport or to some other kind of work or achievement, through which by devious channels they wish to acquire the recognition of sufficiency which they have been denied as far as sex is concerned.
>
> This enormously compelling force which springs from sex is caused by sex vanity and wish for success. There is hardly any single ability or function of man of which he is vainer than his sexual capacity or sufficiency. Therefore frustration which leads to exhibitionism may stimulate every other function or ability and enhance these others more than the thing in itself (nonsexual ability) could ever achieve alone. This enhancement may be in proportion to the frustration; it may also be in appreciation of realization, like the afterglow of sexual intercourse. Lyric poetry, which more than any form of art reflects sexual feeling, shows these two phases frustration and appreciation. Sex, which along with food, etc., is the great life-drive, is much more difficult of realization than any other drive. It exhibits greater variety of effect than anything else in the world, in regard to personality. It is so inextricably mingled with other things that it is difficult to divorce the purely sexual from any moment of life, any activity whatsoever.

In his files, Dreiser often slipped very human little pieces, which might fit into a novel, rather than into a serious study of the universe, as the *Notes* were intended to be. But with Dreiser, all phases of life were valid, if they pointed up some truth, some pathetic or heart-revealing detail. So the following unpublished note is typical of Dreiser's musings:

> How overwhelming the urge not to be alone, to seek companionship. Because of it, the lonely one joins in marriage; the two, still lonely, call in another couple, and the four, still lonely, and in the hope of even a faint touch of kinship before they die, join clubs or follow expeditions—or become politicians, theosophists, dipsomaniacs, or even write or paint. In the city there are those who feel like shadows hurrying along among many shadows. In the country, with one alone but without an emotional response—madness. In the end most will be judged by their hearts. Was he or she moved by that? Did he or she respond? (with what?) Has he, she, a good or kind heart—or one of stone? Is he or she loyal? Fiercely loyal? Can he or she cry? Was either heartbroken? Did the dog cry after his master; mourn over his grave? Sicken and die because he was gone? Why grave stones, memorials, memorial visits? "She is gone! Gone!"

Dreiser's files for the *Notes on Life* contain a number of quotations from the French writer Remy de Gourmont, who had written a sensation-making book, *Physique de L'Amour,* in 1924, later translated as *The Natural Philosophy of Love.* It might better have been called *Sex in Nature,* as it makes an illuminating study of sex life, particularly that of the animal and insect kingdoms. The Frenchman makes the point throughout that "man is an animal," and he wishes to "situate his sexual life on the single plane of a universal sexuality." At the conclusion of his first chapter, he says: "Love is profoundly animal; therein is its beauty."

Such remarks impressed Dreiser greatly. While he did not agree with all of de Gourmont's conclusions, he was amazed at his thorough study of sexual habits of ants, fish, antelopes, and, as a kind of concession, humans. I remember Dreiser's musing over his exposition of polygamy, which is a natural state among all animals, with a few exceptions. De Gourmont wrote:

> The other and true polygamy, polygamy actual, temporary or permanent, is still less rare among people of European civilization, but nearly always secret and never legal; it has for a corollary a polyandry exercised under the same conditions. This sort of polygamy is very different from that of the Mormons, Turks, gallinaceae and antelopes, it is nothing more than promiscuity. It does not dissolve the couple, in diminishing its tyranny it renders it more desirable. Nothing so favours marriage, and consequently, social stability, as the de facto indulgence in temporary polygamy. The Romans well understood this, and legalized concubinage.[13]

The very cynical observations of de Gourmont are almost humorous at times, but his knowledge of biology and sex life makes him a formidable informant, right along Dreiser's line of scientific investigation. The French writer sought the colorful and unusual, as it illuminated both human nature and the universe around him. In the same way, Dreiser was seeking to understand life on every level. So his *Notes on Life* must be understood as his very personal and literary reaction to the facts he gathered, and not as a series of studies from a textbook.

Dreiser could laugh with de Gourmont about polygamy, in his own sardonic way, but facing it in his daily life was another matter. His own practice of polygamy, or varietism as he preferred to call it, was not without qualms of conscience. If not in a religious sense, then out of his personal small voice. He sometimes passed through moods of depression, remorse, coming perhaps from some submerged sense of sin, the sin of doing wrong to others. He knew that he might hurt or deeply wound the woman who was giving him her body because her illusion of love might be stronger than his, or last longer. He realized, from his own life, that a beautiful experience of sexual love can be more devastating to a woman than to a man, who is designed by nature to be less involved in the emotional aftermath of love, and more ready to move on to another. He wanted to create beauty, the full joy and illusion of love, and yet he was caught in tension between the desire to possess and the fear of being possessed, or rather, of having to cope with the jealousy and misery of a possessive woman.

Dreiser might be blamed for his varietism, but hardly a woman who gave herself to him regretted it, because of his innate respect for and appreciation of women in general, and the glow he created around the sexual act, translating passion into love. And what great respect he had for a true love or marriage such as he had not had himself! How he could extol such love, and make it endure beyond the grave! One of his most moving stories, and the one which he said was his favorite, is called "The Lost Phoebe." It describes an aged husband distraught after the death of his wife of many years, going out to search for her behind their ramshackle farmhouse, and seeming to sense her spirit in the foggy wood.[14]

In the fall of 1930, Dreiser returned from a trip to California. I did not see him for some time as I was living at my family home in Connecticut, awaiting the birth of a child. My husband and I had both been highly nervous and this arrangement seemed best, as he could then come up for weekends and I was happy to be in the country. At the end of this period, I came to a New York hospital where my son was born on the 9th of December. Dreiser must have been informed, for he sent me the special edition of his poem,

My City, which had just come out. Accompanying it was a long letter to my child, Hilary, welcoming him to "this best of all possible worlds," a delightful and humorous message of six pages.[15]

After my son's birth, I was critically ill and saw little of Dreiser that winter, although we exchanged several notes. Finally, I had decided to leave the city. My husband and I had still not found the harmony that we had hoped the child and the change of pace might bring. On the contrary, tensions seemed to increase. I was plagued with insomnia and my eyesight seemed threatened. Doctors recommended a complete change. So I obtained passage on a ship, to sail with my small son for Sweden, where I had many relatives, the land of my father.

When Dreiser and I met to say good-bye, it was not without a tearing pain. But much as I had been drawn to him, I felt I could have no part in his life. Helen was the charming hostess who shared his studio, and I was sure he had other women friends as well. He was always secretive about his comings and goings, and although I was not jealous by nature, I did not want to commit myself to any lasting relationship after suffering from my husband's sometimes possessive attitudes toward me. Here was my chance to be free. The fact that Dreiser had been attracted to me, had confidence in me, greatly increased my self-assurance. Also, I felt that he would always be my friend, even from a distance. The world was open to me in a new way.

Dreiser said little that day, or at least that I can remember. His silences were not negative, but brimming with unspoken emotion. Varietist though he was, he would have preferred to have me a little less independent, a little more dependent on him, immobilized by that interest he had turned on me, like a beam from a seeking searchlight. But shaken though I was by his personality, his strength also challenged me to be myself, even though this separation was suddenly and unexpectedly hard and mute.

Perhaps we suffered more than I remember, for his letter to me afterwards was full of a sad self-examination, and an indirect reproach. What had I said to him? Had I boasted of friends who were waiting for me in Sweden, or others here? As I read the letter again and again back then, I wondered why we were so careless with our emotions. Yet he had not written more, nor had he begged me to stay. Certainly the following letter of Dreiser's is testimony to the fact that his own attitude toward sexual freedom was not without afterthought (or forethought). It was not a cynical or superficial defiance of convention, or of consequences, nor a disregard for the sufferings of others, nor again, an escape from suffering for himself. Rather, it was an acceptance of suffering as a price to be paid for that varietism, that restlessness such as St. Augustine described in his *Confessions:* "Thou hast made us restless until we find our rest in Thee." The last part of the letter refers to a novel, *Borealis,* which I had just completed and shown to Dreiser:

December 14, 1930

Dear Marguerite:

I read your letter and in many ways was impressed by it. It is a quality of my mind that it favors every effort toward self-expression and freedom. I have suffered bitterly by that same in others since in many instances it has torn me from them or them from me— and I have bled. But still I favor it. And yet I know also that a condition of such freedom is *self-torture*. One cannot exercise it at the expense of the other fellow alone and unscathed, mentally and emotionally one pays. There are tearing nostalgias in oneself—in me at least—unconquerable, irrepressible vomits of agony. And out of it comes what? Wisdom? Durable and delightful memories? I wish I could be sure. In myself I see isolated strength yet more than that? Peace? Sweetness? Wholeness of heart? A level look into that far amiable land of the heart and all dreams? The future? I wish I could say so. I truly wish. And yet—somehow I am impressed by you and how you do regardless of how reckless or how cruel it looks—at times—or how uncertain the effect—ultimately.

As to your book—it is good in a concentric personal way. I do not feel that it is sufficiently dramatic or in places—especially at the last compelling. And yet I also feel that many should like it. It is good.

As for another one—if you would devise one out of your knowledge of life in general, paint people as you know them—choose your own drama or comedy and illuminate it with your own thoughts and conclusions. Truly I cannot see how it could fail of an audience.[16]

Love from me—who wishes
so much for you—so much real good

T. D.

Dreiser's concern for others was an ever-present trait of his character. Perhaps it began when he felt sorry for his mother in her struggle against poverty. Then he realized that his brothers and sisters, and, in fact, most of the families around them, were in the grip of the same anxiety to survive. They were often cold and hungry, and their neighbors were not much better off. But instead of becoming bitter and resentful, he opened sympathies to all. He did not simply feel sorry for himself.

Later, in his newspaper days, Dreiser offered his heart toward the poor of the big cities, the stream of struggling humanity. He was a reporter who actually suffered over the accidents and wrecks and fires he was sent to cover. And in his own autobiographical writings, some of these calamities come to life, still arousing our sympathies. Such writings led directly toward his becoming a novelist, in order to be able to portray the human condition, as did Balzac, whom he so admired. Dreiser studied people's behavior, particularly that of women, and he investigated working conditions, factories, tenements. Another step took him to social concerns, to politics. The unknown force that created the universe bestowed on man a great many things; perhaps all emotions, passion, compassion, concern for others. Dreiser seemed to have an exuberance of nature which in turn gave him an interest in almost every phase of life, including the political. He is immediately thought of as a political figure because of his polemic writings and his lifelong struggle against injustice and false values. The ruthless power of money in politics both fascinated and appalled him, as he expressed it in his business trilogy, *The Financier, The Titan,* and *The Stoic.*

But how did this interest come about? Not because of any adopted theory of economics, but out of his own experience and nature. I do not need to go into details. Dreiser's own writings are voluminous on the subject. They cover many years of the political scene, going back to World War I. The results of the Great Depression are reflected in *Tragic America,* written not long after *An American Tragedy,* Dreiser's first great financial as well as literary success. Impossible here to cover the efforts, the articles, the activities that took Dreiser's time, involving him in tiring research and keeping him away from the literary tasks he should have concentrated on, had he been striving merely for money or for fame. But he placed concern for human suffering, and the struggle to achieve human rights, far above his personal good. I can add little to the public record of his political idealism, but it may be of interest to describe his life as I saw it, working with him off and on, during the dramatic years of the late thirties and early forties. In the personal story of these days one can see how they were inextricably interwoven with his political activities, and how he never hesitated to sacrifice himself in his concern for others.

Over two years had passed since I left New York to live in Switzerland. When I returned to visit my family during the summer of 1933, I went to see Dreiser—because he was always in the forefront of my mind—and found him in a small suite at the Ansonia Hotel. He asked me what I was doing, and I described my life in Europe, where I was caught up in a round of activities; sports, politics, and romances, moving from Paris to Sweden, but always back to Switzerland where I had developed a passion for climbing its mountains. He listened to me, glowering, and then began to question. I had to admit that I had not had time for much creative work. Then he challenged me to stop wasting my time, and to work for him again. The shock of his personality was overwhelming to me at that moment. Most impelling was the new dedication that I felt in Dreiser to the causes that had always engaged his attention, but now gave him a singleness of purpose.

It was still summertime, and he spent weekends in Mount Kisco at the fantastic new house called Iroki, designed by Ralph Fabri, and roofed with half-logs like a Russian *Isba*.[17] Here Helen had her sister and mother staying with her, as well as two borzoi, one called Nick they had had on Fifty-seventh Street and a mate her sister Myrtle had brought from the West. There were weekend parties, but not quite in the old style. And on Monday mornings, Helen drove Dreiser in to the Ansonia for a working week. At that time he was terminating his work on the *American Spectator,* with its extraordinary roster of editors: George Jean Nathan, Ernest Boyd, James Branch Cabell, Eugene O'Neill, and, of course, Dreiser himself. Sherwood Anderson was a regular contributor.[18] But the very disparity of these talents and the different, slick attitude of Nathan toward the arts and to the downtrodden, whom Dreiser wished to champion, made this combination impossible. Especially since Nathan was in constant opposition to Dreiser. The little help I gave Dreiser in this venture showed me the inner workings of a publication, and in turn gave me the nerve to start a magazine of my own, later on, with Dreiser's encouragement.[19] Other projects, including helping Dreiser with his tremendous correspondence, were valuable experiences. Just to observe the dynamic and compassionate interest he displayed in trying to better the conditions of his day was constantly inspiring.

That autumn, when he still used the address of the *American Spectator,* Dreiser sent me a brief note, typed, with a few lines added by hand about Horace Liveright, who had just died after a time in rather deteriorated circumstances. Dreiser had had bitter battles with him over manuscripts, yet appreciated his knowing charm, and had him as a frequent guest at the big studio parties on Fifty-seventh Street. He now wrote on September 26, 1933: "I attended the Liveright services. They were quite impressive. A really creative if romantic temperament—an aesthetic factor in his day." This seemed to me a noble gesture and comment by Dreiser about someone with whom he had so often quarreled.[20]

Working with Dreiser was an absorbing combination of wanting to please him and being swept into the almost impersonal stream of creation. I believe many who worked for him felt as I did, if they could stand the pace and cared for him enough to persevere. Not that he was such a hard taskmaster, but rather that he himself gave such devotion to his duties, literary, political, and human—response to human need—that it was impossible to be a lukewarm helper. Besides his many writing projects, he tried to answer all his mail, especially from the obscure, the struggling, and the unsuccessful. He never forgot the days of his own poverty and discouragement, and had great concern for human dignity and suffering, everywhere. So it was an inspiration to work for him, a challenge to one's own conscience: "What am I doing to help my fellow man? At the least, I can help Dreiser with what he is doing." And so the days flew swiftly, stretching sometimes into evenings or nights. For when he was tired, then, too, he needed help to relax, to gain perspective on the constant struggle.

But soon the health of my son forced me to go back to Switzerland. Even though I had thought him well off in the country with his grandmother, physically and psychologically, I had neglected him. It would always be so if I were working with Dreiser. The work was too absorbing, Dreiser, too strong. I pulled myself away.

By 1937 storm clouds were gathering over Europe. Mussolini was lord over Italy, and Hitler was beginning to show his hand. My friends in Europe, artists and intellectuals, were all involved in antifascist activities, and I felt it was best to return to America. Two more years in Switzerland had strengthened the little boy, who now went to school. I was eager to arouse or join friends in my own country, who saw the dangers ahead. Then there was always Dreiser. A rock to which one could cling. Coming home, I wrote him a note at Mount Kisco, sure that now in the summer he would be living in his house in the wild fields. Soon I received an answer:

June 8, 1937

Dear Marguerite

Your letter was addressed to Mt. Kisco (Incidentally, welcome home)[.] Helen and I have been living here in N.Y. since Christmas. (Park Plaza Hotel, 50 West 77th St. Endicott 23700)[.] However, Helen has her own room and I have mine. Her's [*sic*] is 1006. Mine is 623. The Mt. Kisco place is rented. I'd be glad to see you here, if your [*sic*] in town, ever. You could drop me a note or we could come out there. I'll explain things when I see you. Are you happy? *More* or *less* Oxfordian? You might write Helen. But you can reach me here by marking the room number 623. It's nice to know your [*sic*] back. Since you say nothing of

Beppie, maybe the Nazis got him. Yes? No? Neither.
Anyhow
Affectionately

T. D.

I'm not passing your note on to Helen.
You write direct as you choose.[21]

When I saw Dreiser in New York, I realized that he was in the midstream of a difficult period in his personal life. A young girl, Harriet Bissel, whom he had engaged to help him with his scientific research, had proved not only efficient but possessed of a quite deadly charm for him, as far as Helen was concerned.[22] Harriet had just graduated with honors from college and had an innate self-assurance. She was flattered that Dreiser was attracted to her, and it could scarcely have been otherwise, for she was as small and pretty as she was clever, with blue eyes set far apart, in a pert, inquiring face. She had long, blond hair and a most disarming smile. But she was too young to handle the situation that arose when she tried to live with Dreiser and Helen, in the Mount Kisco house.

Conflicts had arisen many times before over other women; Dreiser had told Helen years before that she could share his life only if she would yield right of way if he chose to pursue others. Shameless as this sounds, they were not married, and had often lived apart for months at a time. But Helen did not give up easily. Such triangles often developed, and they were always painful for both of them. Violent scenes erupted this time over Harriet. Helen had said she would leave for California, which she had always preferred to New York. But she had not done so. Some weeks after they had rented a house, she finally left to join her mother and sister, in the West.

For a while, Dreiser worked on more peacefully in the city. Times were not peaceful around him, however. The state of our country had always been of the greatest concern to him. He had taken his part in the drama of the Great Depression and fought for the miners of Harlan County.[23] But as conditions improved under the courageous leadership of President Franklin Roosevelt, he had seen a chance to concentrate on his research and formulate a new book. At the time that he had given up the *American Spectator,* he had rejected all other offers because of the project he had in mind, the formulating of his life's philosophy.

The rising menace of war and fascism in Europe had first seemed remote from his immediate work. But the newspaper reports of Hitler's ruthlessness and growing power, the concentration camps, the dive-bombing practice over civilian towns such as Guernica, together with the cynicism of business interests all over the world which seemed to condone Hitler (or at least to partake in the vast and maddening indifference of many in the face of heroic efforts by a few to resist), all this had created a sinister, alarming atmosphere of which Dreiser was increasingly aware. He suffered from it, and we all suffered. There is something like political emotion that is perhaps stronger than any other, when aroused in the negative sense. Not tempered by love but nurtured on hate, it corrodes and causes agonies—pain not directly physical, but mental, impossible to relieve. To care about what was going on. This I had learned from Dreiser, and before I left Europe, I had seen my friends suffering from the same political anger. It was contagious. It became the motivation for my little magazine, *Direction,* and at that time, for my entire life.

Dreiser had been glad to hear about my experiences in Europe and read, with interest, certain reports I had brought back from Paris; new material, confidential information. But all my attempts to persuade him to edit or just to give his name to an antifascist magazine of the arts were in vain. He promised to contribute articles, items, ideas, but he did not want the responsibility of being an editor. However, he did encourage me to start, in a small way, the magazine that seemed to fill an urgent need, and for which many other writers and liberals of the day were eager to provide material. Money seemed secondary in this effort. Somehow it would be found. And so I entered a new phase of my life, not working for Dreiser, but feeling him at my side, with advice and contributions. And sometimes, a rare evening of companionship when it seemed that I could draw from him a dynamic force and love that kept me going.

From our old family home in Connecticut, an hour from the city, I edited *Direction,* a rather shoestring affair. There was plenty of material to be had, and photos, as many as we could use, representing all the arts in the service of the new movement against fascism. There were various organizations in this country dedicated to resisting the spread of totalitarianism or to specifically helping the Spanish people, all of these groups looking for a mouthpiece. The work of the WPA Arts Projects offered fascinating documentary and folk material.[24] Many outstanding writers joined the political struggle and offered articles far below their usual fee. We had the munificent policy of offering one cent per word, and this proved acceptable to men like John Dos Passos, Erskine Caldwell, Kenneth Burke, and many others. With little help, and less money, I rushed into a fertile field of action. Commuting almost every day to the city, I met authors and editors in their offices, or in hotel lobbies, in the Museum of Modern Art, or in the Grand Central Station. But at least my official abode was fixed.

Now Dreiser entered on a period of disruption, moving from place to place. Places, places, places. I paraphrase his way of repeating a word three times to hold its image. But at that period, it was more like an image of no-place for him, no chance to settle down with his papers, a small comfort for work, an address and a phone. Like going back to the old days of poverty, the anonymous rooms in boarding houses or ramshackle apartments in the Village. Then had come the truly splendid studio on Fifty-seventh Street, and the Mount Kisco places, first the white birch cabins followed by the big home with the log roof built at its master's command. Now the strange, romantic house was rented and up for sale. He had tried to live in the smaller addition, in the cabins on the property, but they could not give him the peace and stability he needed. Fortunately, at that time, Dreiser's friend Calvin Bridges, by whose side he had spent the summer once at Woods Hole Marine Biological Laboratory, was now about to continue his research at the Marine Laboratory of Cold Spring Harbor on Long Island.[25] Bridges suggested that Dreiser and Harriet join him there. Dreiser could get a large, comfortable room, and live most inexpensively in the community of scientists, which he found very agreeable. He wrote to me from Cold Spring Harbor, saying that he thoroughly enjoyed the place and that he was "reverent" and "deeply respectful" in the presence of the biologists. He also described a picnic or clambake on the beach, and this whole experience made a happy summer of work and useful observation for him. It was at Cold Spring Harbor at this time that he noticed a small bunch of yellow flowers, as he came from the laboratories, and saw in them the same design that he had been admiring under the microscope. This was a step in his slow approach to the vision of a Creator.[26]

But when the summer was over, he must move again. He first went back to the hotel where he had spent the winter, but as his following letter tells, he was miserably crowded there. He then found a charming apartment on Eleventh Street, in a house where he had actually lived some twenty years before, with his sister Mame. There was a large living room which ran the length of the house, with a garden in the rear and trees and lovely long vines in front, framed by a wrought-iron balcony. A small hall-bedroom, kitchen, and bath were adequate for his simple style of living. He worked well here all winter. I had helped him to move and lent him some paintings and rugs, and hated to see him give up this place when spring came. However, he wished to see if he could live at Mount Kisco once more, since his tenants had left, and he knew that it would only be a question of time before the place was sold. The two following letters refer to the beginning and to the end of these days:

October 1, 1937

Dear Marguerite:

I would have called you yesterday but I was disappointed in my moving arrangements. I am taking a place for awhile (by the month) at 116 West 11th St.—an old house in which a sister of mine once lived. And I too. I was to have gone in today. Now I may not get in until the 4th or 5th,—the person now in it claiming the privilege of staying until then. When I do move I'd appreciate your help. Harriet is quite ill. A diseased appendix on the right side and an ovarian cist [*sic*] on the other required two operations. It may be two months before she is really well and able to work again. Meantime I'm troubled with a lot of things she looked after with ease and skill. Yesterday I removed all my belongings from Cold Spring Harbor and now am jammed into 1 room here since I gave notice a week ago and they rented my suite. The hotel is full. However if I may I'll call you and if you're free I'll be obliged.

It's lovely weather and I'd so much rather be in Cold Spring Harbor than here. Sorry you didn't get to see it.

All my best wishes.

T. D.

April 7, 1938

Dear Marguerite:

I'm moving back to Mt. Kisco today—really in order to put the place in shape for the summer. *This* telephone will be disconnected this P.M. and my new telephone will be the same as always at Mt. Kisco—5413. I'm not sure that I'll be up there for any great length of time—not if I can rent or sell it. Nearly all of my stuff has already gone. I have here your three pictures, your two rugs; a blanket belonging to you and two or three pillows. I'll take them along and shortly deliver them to you at Darien.[27] And I am grateful to you for giving me the use of them for so long. They aided much in making the place cheerful.

Just now the latest number of *Direction* came. You seem able to scout out all of the latest cultural and socio-political developments or the outlook for the same and condense them so that they can be quickly grasped. What ever [sic] you do though don't make it too speedy. If you leave your readers breathless it is possible to leave quite a few of them behind. *I* like it, though. Is it going? Needless to say I hope so.

Regards. And if you have any free country time drop over some afternoon.

T. D.

Address me Mt. Kisco.

Dreiser's move to Mount Kisco proved impractical, because the big house was soon rented and the cabins had no running water. The higher cabin presented a climb that Dreiser found tiring, and the lower cabin, built into the hillside, still more primitive with its dirt floor and too-large fireplace, was dangerously damp. Again, Dreiser was homeless. Helen kept urging him to come to California, but he was still not ready to do so. He kept doggedly on with his work, and Harriet was constantly turning up new material for him to examine. His files were now bursting with papers. Where could he keep them? Since I was often in touch with him, because of the magazine, I offered to let him use a small house I had rented as a daytime swimming place, for the summer, near my home. Here my son enjoyed a sandy beach and had companions to play with, while I often typed away on the porch, taking a quick dip now and then, when the tide was in. We called this place "The Shack," but at least it had running water, a shower, a small kitchen with a woodstove for chilly evenings—much

Marguerite Tjader at "The Shack." Photo courtesy of Hilary Harris

more comfortable than Dreiser's cabins. He had seen the place and liked it, so he agreed to try it out.

May 23, 1938

Dear Marguerite:

Thanks for the offer. And you know that I appreciate it fully. Whether I can occupy it by the month or not now—I don't know. I have a number of things I must do in N.Y. in June and have been thinking I'd stay a part of the time anyhow down there in a hotel. However, next Wednesday I have to leave here and I haven't had time—and won't have to pick my hotel at once. I thought, if it is alright with you that I'd use your cabin from Wednesday to Monday A.M. or—noon—then go down to whatever place I have selected. After that, and if your [*sic*] not using it, I'd be glad to pay a monthly rate for the partial use of it—because after all you do have to pay for it and it is a lovely place to go. The only reasons I don't take it flat—the need for attending to a number of things—and conveniently in N.Y. (You have no phone out there) and next because I fear the neighbors might possibly get too hilarious weekdays—when I am trying to concentrate. So the other way might be better for me. But you decide what you must—

You know, Marguerite, I care for you a lot and always have. Your a swell guy—to me—and I notice that others think so. I like being near you. Be good and retain your affection and friendship for me.

T. D.

I was delighted to have Dreiser nearby. His letter showed some misgiving, but as it turned out, he was quite happy at "The Shack" for the month of June and half of July, when the dramatic mission of going to beleaguered Barcelona was offered to him. In the relative peace and sunny quiet of my cabin, the challenge of going to Spain, where the Republican armies were making a last stand around Barcelona, came as a great shock to Dreiser. He had just begun to relax with a swim on the beach every day and hours of meditative work on his *Notes on Life*. It had seemed as if now at last, he could get ahead with the slow formation of his original and very personal philosophy. But his life had never flowed smoothly, and now it was presented to him that this might be a last chance to arouse the world to what was going on—not only in Spain, but in Europe, as Mussolini shamelessly sent his armed men to fight on the side of the rising dictator, Franco. And Hitler's growing air force was beginning to practice its latest methods of dive bombing on the ragged, exhausted army of Republican Spain. Guernica and other villages had been mercilessly bombed, and now Barcelona.

But at that time, in August 1938, all was not lost. It seemed the gesture that Dreiser was asked to make might send up a flare against the whole black picture of growing fascism and the still more diabolical Nazi power. So, old newspaperman and crusader that he was, Dreiser went off at two days' notice. He was asked to stop in Paris on the way, to address a conference against the bombing of open cities and he was given a first-class reservation on *The Normandie*. Here he found several passengers whom he knew well, as he related in a letter to me from the boat. To cut this personal letter would subtract some of its vitality. Serious as Dreiser was, there was always time for the light touch, and for unrelated events that caught his imagination—Howard Hughes (who died as the billionaire recluse) was then at the top of his career. He had just made his sensational flight around the world in four days. But more sinister feats of science were threatening humanity—rockets, dive-bombers, fire-bombing, the holocaust of World War II:

July 15, 1938

I was thrilled by Howard Hughes doing it in 4 days!

a bord, *le Normandie*

Dear Marguerite:

Won't you pardon my not telephoning you. There were so many things to do. As Harriet could tell you I almost fell on the boat. Money to arrange for—exchange. A ticket to be ordered from Paris by cable and picked up by me at the dock. (Delay, delay, delay.) My passport. Necessary clothes to get together. A conference dinner to attend. Newspaper men and photographers. And no sooner was I on and ready to send a telegram the very last call was being enforced—crowds being pushed off. Not a telegraph boy left: Only cablegrams.

And since then labors—looking over documents sent me and conferring with fellow committeemen on board—and correspondents. And running into—of all people—Madam Clayburgh. Main cabin 335 and having a lot of people I must meet. Charles J. and John O'Hara Cosgrave—the old Sunday Editor of N.Y. World and his wife. And Marian Powys and her boy Peter enroute to Paris and England to see Llewellyn and Jack, and right around the corner from me. And Sam Groskopf—a learned German Jew thrown out of Germany and living in Paris and wanting to tell me all about [it]. And then letters to write—to my bank, to Golden, to Helen, to Hume, my publisher—to a lot of people I must see in Paris.[28] And now to you.

How very nice you have been to me! And how truly appreciative! If I thought I were the man to stand all your eager, zestful, passionate goings on I'd move in with you (per invitation of course) only I fear the neighbors would never endure the uproar. But you are so swell and interesting and vivid. And will always be so I think. I'll never forget the first time I sat beside you at Tish's table and how exquisite you looked—and were. Ah, me!

Anyhow this is to say I'm sorry I didn't telephone you, because I wanted to.

And that I think of you plenty and wish you every good thing—most truly—most of all to be happy because you honestly try to make other people happy.

So there, beloved. And send me a few kind thoughts. I don't intend to stay any longer than I need to. It's hard work and I don't love to travel like you do. I wish I did. But if you were here we'd make out because I'd unload all this social stuff on you and I don't mean maybe. So love and good wishes. I'll put you in my prayers.

T. D.

My Paris address for the time being is c/o E. C. Llewellynn, 18 Place Vendome. And mail will be picked up or forwarded. Love to Harriet. But don't show her this . . . and explain to Barbara how swiftly I had to beat it.

In Paris Dreiser made an address entitled "Equity Between Nations." It was later published in *Direction,* and it emphasized Dreiser's concept of *equity*. He described the conference to me as putting him in a very difficult position, as certain leaders, knowing his views, refused to call on him. But he waited out his time, and came forward, when they could no longer ignore him. He spoke with great patience, as he still hoped that he could have some impact on reactionary elements present. His text called for the world to adopt the values in the U.S. Constitution with its assumption of a "fifty-fifty" sharing of available resources. It lamented the tendency of certain individuals to wish to be "giants in a world that consists only of little men," and "to struggle for enormous individual wealth and enormous individual power." Instead we should all realize that we are "co-heirs of all that is." Dreiser ended this moving speech with an emotional exhortation that the world try "a few hundred years of the Brotherhood of Man."[29]

Dreiser's speeches and political writings may seem dated, since they refer to events long past. But just because they come from his deep well of understanding for human beings, they are a part of all that great body of political literature that keeps the record of history better than newspapers or schoolbooks. They bring back the contemporary scene in all its urgency. They may be naive in their belief in good will. And in his way of oversimplifying the basic condition of society as one of inequity. In his implying that fair play between nations, between capital and labor, and between individuals who might be persuaded to curb their greed and struggle for power, would bring about equity. But he believed deeply in the rights of individuals.

Alas, Dreiser knew only too well that many other elements, ruthless and political, were involved. And yet the call to justice must be made in every age, every generation, regardless of whether it is answered. The conscience of mankind has slowly begun to develop. Mediation, instead of war, the responsibility of sharing the food and resources of the world, have at last become accepted concepts, since Dreiser's day.

But he was speaking on the very eve of the Second World War. It could have been avoided. Hitler could have been stopped, through the cooperation of the great powers. But there was money to be made. Business interests in all countries were callous about human suffering and hoped that fascism would cancel itself out in a death struggle with communism. Nations were divided into left and right, as they are today. The fascinating, devilish game of politics played on. Dreiser was truly not interested in parties or politics for their own sake. If he was a leftist, it was because he was for the have-nots. The deep sense of injustice that he had concerning our society was the product of his own struggles with poverty and then the endless observations he made of the whole human scene around him. Like Dickens in nineteenth-century England, Dreiser, in all his novels, had become the spokesman for the American poor whom he loved.

Consider his so-called political books, like *Tragic America* or *America Is Worth Saving.*[30] Here again, Dreiser was the humanist, the lover of mankind rather than the politician. The plight of miners in Kentucky or the discomfort of the slum-dwellers in cold-water flats in Harlem or East Side New York haunted him. The figure of a thinly clad man hurrying along a side street or the sad face of a woman in a cafeteria might bring tears to his eyes. All this was a part of Dreiser, the "political animal." He went his own way, politically as well as romantically and philosophically. His integrity was that of a Rodin statue, rough-hewn, and colossal, standing firm for what he believed and felt, not according to any theory, but animated by the passion of his heart. One might call it political love, as important as any other variety, perhaps more so.

When Dreiser risked his life to go to Barcelona, the Republican cause was nearly lost. He had talked to various leaders and seen the plight of that "open city" in which he had survived two bombings. There was nothing more that he could do but share the defeat of the heroic Spanish people, as Ernest Hemingway, André Malraux, and others of the Lincoln Brigade who fought with guns, as well as by their writings and speeches, had been forced to do. On his return to Paris, Dreiser found a cynical attitude, in spite of messages he bore, and his own report. He then went on to England, for an equally discouraging interview with Churchill.[31] The only interlude which gave him a respite and some pleasure was his spontaneous visit to Corwen in Wales to see his old friend, John Cowper Powys. Since Powys was such an important figure in Dreiser's life, perhaps the reader will forgive me if I interject at this point an account of the friendship between these two literary lions.

Throughout his life, Dreiser had strong friendships with men, and many of them are described by his biographers or in his own writings. There was Arthur Henry, of the newspaper world, who recognized Dreiser's ability as a reporter. Both sensitive, struggling journalists in a rough world, they became fast friends. Later, there was George Sterling, the poet of San Francisco. Edgar Lee Masters became his friend during his days in Chicago, and their affection endured throughout the years. As late as 1943 when Edgar's health was failing, Dreiser showed him affectionate concern.[32]

Impossible to mention all the varied types and characters who were a part of Dreiser's life. Many he has described himself. He enjoyed personalities as different as Charles Fort, the self-styled philosopher, obsessed by the strange facts and events he had collected all of his life, and Paul Robeson, the great singer who had come to Dreiser for encouragement in his Greenwich Village days, when he was rehearsing for his first play, *The Emperor Jones,* and the acerbic critic, H. L. Mencken.[33]

But it may be that Dreiser's greatest, most enduring friendship was with the extraordinary Welshman, writer, and lecturer, Powys. From 1913, his life paralleled Dreiser's and in their affinity, they threw light on each other. Powys first met Dreiser at the time when *The 'Genius'* was being berated by the press, and Powys came thundering to his defense in his lectures, declaring he had encountered no other American writer like him.[34] Indeed, I can testify to Powys's extraordinary power as a lecturer, having listened to his untamed and passionate arguments on several occasions. I sat in my seat, trembling, shaken by the force of his ideas, of the possibilities of literature sweeping over me like great music, but most of all by this personality, of a kind that hypnotized and exalted. At the time I met Dreiser, Powys had a small, cold-water flat on the tiny square, Patchin Place, in Greenwich Village. He preferred this to steam heat and kept his fire going briskly in an old blackened hearth. He wore heavy English tweeds and always carried a gnarled blackthorn cane. The two men walked together, or talked when they had time. There is little record that they saw each other often; rather their affinity was something timeless. Powys has expressed their mutual affection in his autobiography:

> I used to be aware—I am always aware—of surging waves of magnetic attraction between Dreiser and myself, waves which certainly are not homosexual, for neither of us has the remotest homosexual tendency, but which seem superchemical and due to the diffusion of some mysterious, occult force through the material envelopes of our physical frames. The truth is, Dreiser and I are both Magicians. We are two lamas, who, while understanding black magic and the ways of black magicians, prefer for reasons rather to be concealed than revealed, to practice white magic. We both have morbidly active consciences. Problems of right and wrong are far more important to us than problems of aesthetics. Of course there are endless intellectual and moral fields where he leaves me far behind, such as knowledge of economics, appreciation of music, courage in standing up to personal enemies, courage in defying brutal and stupid authorities, freedom from the vice of flattery, integrity of *speech* as well as of mind. But I think the most important item, speaking as a fellow-lama or fellow-guru, where I beat Dreiser at our spiritual "game of wrists," is my power of escaping from the world. But on the other hand since my tendency to escape from the world is largely composed of *fear of the world* and Dreiser's tendency to stay in the world is very largely mingled with a desire to fight for "the insulted and injured" of the world, I am not in a position to take much moral unction to myself concerning this advantage.

In another connection, he said: "All my life I shall at intervals call up the fascinating personalities of Dreiser and Masters, and bless my stars that it has been my destiny to know such men and name myself their friend."[35]

From Patchin Place, Powys moved to a small farmhouse-cottage in a valley near Hartsdale, New York, about a hundred miles from the city. With his fascination for odd words, he named it "Pfudd's Bottom." He had found an ideal companion in a small, frail woman from Kansas, who had a lovely, haunting face. Perhaps his heroine in *Wolf Solent* had some of her quality.[36] Dreiser and Helen, when they were at Mt. Kisco, often visited Jack and Phyllis, and they made a happy foursome. But Powys longed for his native land, and they sold the house at Pfudd's Bottom in 1934, much to Dreiser's regret. Powys always remembered the beautiful Helen of those days, who drove the car, which none of the others cared to do, and who had a disarmingly charming smile and chuckle. He also admired Nick, the Russian wolfhound who always came along and chased the rabbits in the valley.

Dreiser had not seen Jack for several years when he stopped to visit him on his way home from Barcelona in 1938, but they exchanged letters from 1914 on. On his way to Spain on *The Normandie,* Dreiser had found Jack's sister, Marian, on the boat, with her son, Peter. They were on their way to visit Jack in Wales, and urged Dreiser to stop off on his return trip.

After his most disheartening experience in Barcelona, Dreiser was glad to do so. Marian and Peter were still there when he came, and they witnessed the happy reunion of these two wild spirits.

A letter that Powys had written Dreiser in the middle thirties, prepared him for the simple life Jack led in Wales.

No Date

September is about the best of all months in England—warm, hazy, misty, windless, enchanted weather—heavy mist over sea and land in the early morning, and then misty, sometimes, all day.

As I write this now on my couch, Phyllis has gone with the village carrier to Dorchester to see about the papering and painting of our flat, and putting in a sink. I can hear at this moment the moaning sound like that of a great sea beat on the light stick on the Shambles Rock because of the fog.

I relish well going over the hill in the early morning, making a dark track as the cattle do, through the heavy, whitish dew, to get gorse-prickles and furze sticks and thorn sticks and elder sticks to light our fire. (It's pretty primitive.)[37]

Dreiser told me that on his stopover in Wales after the Barcelona trip he had found Jack in a small stone house with Phyllis and the dog, "Very Old," an ancient, uncouth spaniel who would sulk, slink, or simply disappear until Jack called to him. Then he would come like a shot from under some bed or table. But the dog never paid attention to any other person. Jack was living as simply as any retired Welsh farmer. His luxury was the long walk which he took each day, with one of his huge gnarled canes and "Very Old." Usually wrapped in a rough greatcoat or tweed cape, Powys was the unforgettable figure he had always been to Dreiser. Their walks together, at various times in the past, as now, partook of the nature of some earthy pagan or mystic rite. A fellowship of two satyrs, half-gods stalking upon low shoulders of Olympus. Dreiser related that once when they had been walking together on a mountain near Los Angeles, Jack had suddenly stopped and exclaimed over some tiny wildflowers, and swore that they were like some that grew on the English moors, the very same. To Dreiser they looked quite ordinary, but to Jack they were rare, fragrant, of infinite importance and delight. He was excited by them as if he had discovered gold, said Dreiser, so deeply moved, because they stirred in him the love of his own country, his native heath.

Now as they walked over the lanes in Wales, coming quickly out of the little town into rich countryside, full of legend and meaning for Powys, he began to tell Dreiser of his forebears; this was the land from which they sprang. Yes, he would show Dreiser the very place where some of them had lived and died, or passed into the spirit world. For he sensed that some of them were still here on the moors at night.

They passed into a beautiful wooded section, over some stretch of a familiar estate, when, suddenly they were stopped by the gentleman-owner, and told they were trespassing! Powys explained with his best eloquence who he was; how his ancestors had lived here, and that the man with him was Theodore Dreiser, the greatest American writer, visiting him for this brief day. But the owner only glowered the more fiercely, and ordered them off, like a pair of old tramps!

Dreiser was hugely amused by this incident and told of it with tears of laughter in his eyes. What he treasured most out of his whole unhappy trip to Europe was this visit with Jack, to see him with Phyllis and Very Old, with Jack's ancestors hovering nearby; as near contentment as such a great spirit, earthbound, can come. Perhaps never after that visit did Dreiser have such equal fellowship.

As Dreiser approached New York on the Cunard liner *Laconia,* after his interlude with Powys, he was interviewed by newspaper men who had boarded in Boston. He had a contract for several articles and was to make a speech shortly after arrival. Even if it might now be too late to help Republican Spain, the American people must know what had happened and be made aware of the dangers that lay ahead. The day before he arrived, this letter came to me from the *Laconia*. I found that he was to be met officially, and that a suite was reserved for him at the George Washington Hotel, near Gramercy Park:

August 19, 1938

Dear Marguerite:

Back, or will be Monday noon. Just now off the Newfoundland Banks. Had a hard, quick, busy trip—France, Spain, England, Wales. And conferred with many interesting people. Have a Spanish government commission. When I get in I think I'll go to the Ansonia until I straighten things out. Expect Harriet to meet me but am never sure, but Pier 54 is not far from the Ansonia & I have little luggage. I hope you are OK. I would have written but writing was almost impossible. Mostly notes, phone calls, telegrams, taxis, trains. This boat has given me my first rest. But I'll be seeing you. Europe is like [a] rumbling crater. I fear war is much nearer than people think. If Chamberlain is forced out it will [come] I think.[38]

Anyhow love and best wishes.

T. D.

A difficult task lay ahead for Dreiser, and also a heart-rending one.

Only those close to him in those days could see what a heavy toll this trip had taken on his energy and peace of mind. Above all, it was the people of Spain who had earned his admiration and who haunted him. He was granted an audience with President Roosevelt, who also felt sympathy for Spain. The president proposed that Dreiser get together a committee to support him, if he raised the embargo on shipments to Spain, which was then in effect. But again, most civic leaders he could reach in New York were cynical or indifferent as those in France and England.

However, it was because of this effort that Dreiser met the great Quaker, Rufus Jones, who was head of the American Friends Service Committee, which sent humanitarian help to both sides in Spain to aid the suffering soldiers and civilians. In Jones, Dreiser encountered a man of his own stature who illustrated the real meaning of the religious term "Friend." Dreiser had studied Quaker tenets as he had formulated *The Bulwark,* the novel long in his mind, about a family of Friends. He told Jones of his half-finished project, and Jones gave him a book on his own youth which was an invaluable help and inspiration to Dreiser when he finally was able to turn back to the novel.[39] And when we later worked on *The Bulwark* together, Dreiser told me that if he ever were tempted to adopt any one religion, it would be that of the Friends, with their emphasis on justice and the Inner Light.

But at that time in 1938, in New York, how could Dreiser write or even think deeply in the welter of details and demands around him? The following note, written at the George Washington Hotel in New York, reflects his state of mind. His favorite sister, Mame, was dying of a heart condition; Harriet had left him because of problems of her own.[40]

September 6, 1938

Marguerite Dear:

Monday was impossible. I had contracted for four articles with George Bye—delivery this A.M. And they have just gone off now. Also I have a splitting headache—due to working until 11:30 P.M. yesterday midnight. And I would have given anything to be there. Also at 2:30 I had a hurry call from my sister Mame in Astoria who is always troubled with her heart. Think she is going. I had to go over there. And I've three other damned jobs right ahead of me on the table. If I could only come out some afternoon. You wouldn't pick me up at the train would you? I'd like to come alone?

Just now I found the old unpaid bill. I know you had to pay it, so please cash this check and be kind to dumb fools. Meantime I have to work.

Love,

T. D.

I spent as many hours as I could trying to help and cheer Dreiser, but I was almost desperate myself, for want of time and money, as I tried to bring out *Direction.* This was no time to give up the antifascist struggle and Dreiser had given me much original material from Spain. In the meantime, Helen kept writing, urging Dreiser to come to California. Certainly, he could not go back to Mount Kisco alone, and in the winter. The house there was not sold, however, and his furniture and papers were hardly safe left unattended. In one of his sudden decisions, Dreiser engaged professional packers who could send files, furnishings, and artworks to Hollywood. He himself stayed on at the George Washington Hotel. He was winding up his political commitments. The situation in Europe was growing more ominous, and Hitler was about to invade Czechoslovakia.

The night of September 21, 1938, a hurricane from the Caribbean roared up the eastern coast and hit New York as night was falling. Some of us were attending a large rally addressed by the brother of Edward Benes, then premier in Prague.[41] As the storm broke, the lights went out in the auditorium. At the same moment came the news, over a croaking radio, that Czechoslovakia had been invaded by the Nazis. On the darkened stage, a strong voice called out for calm. "The lights in this hall will soon be on again . . . but in my country, they have gone out forever!" An unforgettable moment of political emotion.

The next day, when I returned to my home in the country, I could hardly get through to my old house, about two miles from the railroad station. Trees sprawled across the road; wires were down. It was another day before I could drive down to see what had happened to "The Shack." A week later, Dreiser wrote the following letter and I was able to tell him what had happened. Fortunately, all his papers had been removed.

October 3, 1938

Dear Marguerite:

Did the house blow away? Or what? Was anything injured? I tried to reach you one day by telephone, but you were not in—only expected later. Incidentally, I'd like to know this. After I left [on the trip to Spain] did Harriet remove all of my papers and books from the place or did she forget some things? I would like to know because I miss several volumes and some manuscripts. Did you remove anything to Tokenique?[42] Will you let me know. I'll be greatly obliged.

How are you? I've been so rushed. And still am. But I wish I might come out someday before I leave. Also I hope all goes well.

Love,

T. D.

Dreiser wanted to see "The Shack," and I took him down a few days later. He had loved this little place, where he had at least a few weeks of peace and beauty. We spoke of the guests we had gathered on some occasions; Edgar Lee Masters, Olin Downes, Art Young, Gilbert Wilson, Dorothy Dudley, and others.[43] And we spoke of the days when we had been alone, swimming, laughing, carefree.

Then we went back to my mother's big house, with its wide veranda and view of the water, framed by rocks and trees.[44] Here Dreiser had a large room, and sank quietly into the comfort of the old family abode. He sensed the life that had transpired here for some thirty years, the departed Viking father, the mother gracious still, though in her seventies; the five children who had grown up, married, and gone on, yet leaving their imprint with that of the many relatives and religious characters whom my mother always gathered around her. A very lived-in house, said Dreiser, and he was happy there. Once more, he came for a weekend, and much later, he wrote in a letter: "Tired as I am, I would love to pack my bag and return. I even think of renting a room of you at your country place!"

But in the fall, he finally pulled up his last stakes in the East. He went to California where Helen was waiting for him, to find a house for the familiar furniture, the files, the artworks, and the plaster head of John Cowper Powys.

At "The Shack" with visitors; Edgar Lee Masters, second from left; Dreiser, second from right. Photo courtesy of Hilary Harris.

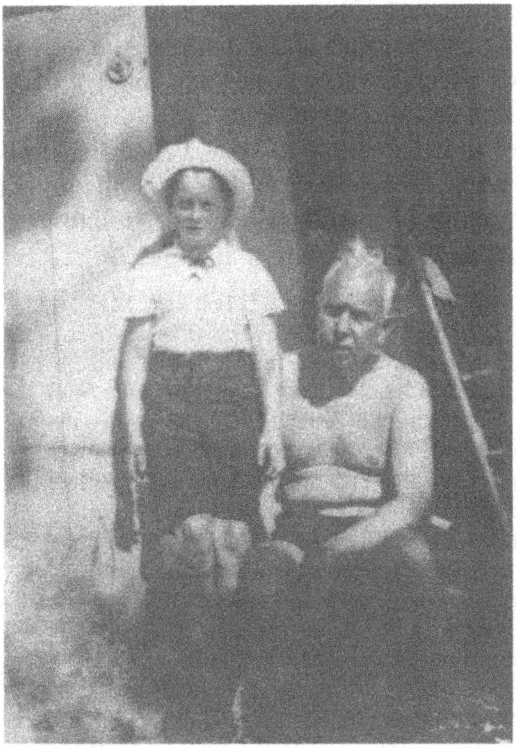

Hilary Harris and Theodore Dreiser. Photo courtesy of Hilary Harris

The last stressful effort on Dreiser's part to fight in the political arena was his brief appearance in New York during February of 1941. He had been invited to come to New York to launch his book *America Is Worth Saving,* and to speak at a formal dinner in the city, and also to address a large rally in Newark, New Jersey. This was the curious period before Pearl Harbor, when many Americans from Norman Thomas, the socialist, to Charles Lindbergh, the flyer, left-wingers and right-wingers, radicals and pacifists, were trying to keep our country from entering the battlefield for widely different reasons. The situation was as challenging as it was confusing. True to his old fighting spirit, Dreiser had been persuaded to leave the quiet of his new Hollywood home. It was a Moorish-type stucco house on a wide street of lawns and palms.[45] Here Helen was taking care of him and trying to keep disturbances away so that he could complete his long-planned novel, *The Bulwark*. With the help that Rufus Jones had given him with his own book depicting his early childhood, Dreiser had started to write a new introduction to the Quaker story. He was also working to assemble his *Notes on Life,* and put some of them in article form to sell to magazines, as he was extremely low on funds at this period. And he was also trying to formulate ideas for screenplays, since he knew many professionals in the glamorous capital of the movie industry.[46]

Then suddenly he had been urged to come to New York, and I was asked to serve as his secretary while he would be in the city. Of course, I was delighted at the prospect of seeing him again, and wrote to tell him so. Soon I received the following note, on Dreiser's new stationery.

February 12, 1941

Dear Marguerite:

Surprised but glad that you are to look after things for me while I'm there. Plan to arrive morning of Feb. 28. Either by New York Central or plane from Chicago. Will let you know. Would like a room at the Commodore, since the first talk is to be in that hotel. You'll find me there if you give me [sic] my room number. I'm travelling light. Don't know that I care to invite many. Edgar Lee Masters and his girl friend at the Chelsea Hotel. Also Harriet (now Mrs. . . .). As for services—I judge you, as the Committee's liason [*sic*] officer, will be handing me directions to my various speaking places. Also departing and arriving times. You sound as vigorous and active as ever so I don't need to say how are you. As soon as my engagements are over I intend to beat it west since lots of work hangs over my head here. But I'll enjoy having you near while I'm there.

Solemnly and respectfully,

T. D.

When Dreiser arrived in New York, he strode across the Grand Central Station, as though he had never left. He loved this city and had always felt a part of it, since his early newspaper days. Ups and downs had never made him change his appreciation of its drama and contrasts, since he had written his first impressions in *The Color of a Great City.*[47] Looking out of the eleventh-floor windows of his suite at the Commodore, he wanted me to sit by him, to enjoy this return. But the telephone began ringing. Newsmen were waiting to interview him. His first duty was a huge dinner and speech at the Commodore, with many controversial elements present. Dreiser was forceful as usual, and very much on the defensive about his new book *America Is Worth Saving*. His old zeal for justice had been aroused once more. However, this time, the issues were not so clear. History was on the move. A position valid one day had changed the next. To describe the situation now is as difficult as it was for Dreiser at that time, surrounded by his friends and also by angry critics. We all shared the tensions of those days. Dreiser actually suffered from them, as he had suffered over Spain. He was gruffer than ever when forced into arguments and duties beyond his strength.

When we were alone he told me that he was also depressed about his life in California. His work was not going well; he had been distracted by his political book and the revised introduction to *The Bulwark* had not impressed his editor at Putnam.[48] His financial situation was worse than ever. The only happy thing he had to relate was that he had found a new friend whom he described as a charming and talented woman named Elizabeth. She had come to Hollywood to write screenplays for which she had some experience.[49]

The days flew by so fast that there was little I could do to lighten Dreiser's mood. I was torn between the task of editing *Direction* from my home, arranging appointments for Dreiser, and catching trains. There were few hours for rest or companionship. Soon, the whole interlude was over, before it had fully begun.

An unforgettable memory of that period was Dreiser's powerful speech to the factory workers of Newark, attended by many of his close friends, who had made the trip out to New Jersey to hear him. Contrasting with his speech at the dinner given in the Commodore Hotel, which had been delayed to the point where Dreiser was tired and overly emotional because of the many drinks set before him, this talk was an expression of the great novelist at his dynamic best. I wish that there could have been a tape made of his impassioned evocation of "the power of the people" which he felt was inherent in the working class.

Alas, no one knew better than Dreiser that the mass is an unpredictable force, but that did not mar the concept of its potential magnificence when rightly motivated and directed. It was the potential that Dreiser was expounding that evening in terms of rare eloquence. But this occasion also took a tremendous toll of Dreiser's strength. He had swept his audience into an emotion comparable to that evoked by the ending of a great symphony. But he, the conductor, was shaken and exhausted. I wish the symphony could be played again, as I can remember it in my own mind. It could well go down as a symbol of Dreiser as crusader.

A few months later came Pearl Harbor. The indisputable necessity for defending ourselves against Hitler and fascism, and their Japanese allies, swept away all hesitancy to fight. Dreiser, like everyone else, was now engaged in a clear-cut struggle against what seemed like evil incarnate. But this struggle in no way changed his mind about the need for love. That need was inherent in Dreiser's nature. He would be the last to say that he followed any theory or pattern of behavior, yet his emotional nature was balanced by his drive for work, for taking a part in the struggles of his day, and by his tireless quest for facts and truth. This indicated a different kind of love, of which he had need as much as of sexual love, at the other end of the spectrum.

Perhaps there is a key to this need of both kinds of love in Dreiser's own personality. There was about him a warm, vibrant quality, as if he were brimming over with some kind of hidden force. Describing this characteristic of Dreiser's for those who did not know him is difficult. But many of his friends, and especially women, were aware of it. What was this intensity that sometimes seemed to consume him, as it did others around him? Was it a quality of mind, or magnetism, or the emanation of some creative or psychic current that came from him, or perhaps through him as he would prefer to think of it, the operation of the Creative Spirit or Life-process itself?

It was, at any rate, something that required reciprocity.

On the spiritual level, this need for love and to love may have been the very source of his drive to know, to search, to respond. On the physical plane, it could be found through the love of women. In this twofold sense, the spiritual and physical, I would like to add to the record through letters and personal accounts.

For many years, if Dreiser met a woman who appealed to him in face or figure, he immediately thought of her in romantic terms. He would approach her in his intense but smiling manner and speak to her, get her to express herself to him. Five minutes later, he might have lost interest, if her temperament did not respond to his. But if he sensed a rapport, he would suggest a meeting without further delay. In the emotional turmoil of his studio days (the big studio on Fifty-seventh Street, where I had first met him) women ran after him, not only because of his personal magnetism, or his new fame after the publication of *An American Tragedy,* but because of the rare understanding of men and women, shining in all his novels. Even men were drawn to his work as aficionados who found in him something that helped them understand their own wives and also themselves.

Dreiser told me that a couple had once written him such an exceptional letter of appreciation that he accepted an invitation to visit them for an evening in their New Jersey home. They came for him in their car. It developed that both husband and wife had really fallen in love with him, through his work. They were intellectual as well as highly emotional types. She was a very handsome woman and her husband seemed proud to offer her to Dreiser. He stayed with her for the night, feeling strange about the situation. But the husband insisted that he had done them a great honor. And he never forgot this attractive and articulate couple who said that he had enriched their lives.

Dreiser preferred to make his own conquests and surround them with mystery, however. He had learned that if beauty were to be created, there must be psychological understanding as well as physical attraction. His lust had not always waited for this, but in later years he had begun to acquire sexual wisdom. He did not want to mar love by angles of possessiveness or jealousy. Perhaps Dreiser was too creative in his relationships, his involvement turning sex too easily into love. Or at least a semblance of love. This was what made women respond to him so readily and yet, no doubt, many suffered more than they gained when they found that they could not have the warmth and immediacy of his presence exclusively for themselves.

In her remarkably frank and honest book, *My Life with Dreiser,* Helen described her own sufferings and jealousies because of his interest in many women, yet she had been obliged to understand that scenes and anger, even though they made Dreiser suffer too, would not change his desire for freedom of action.[50] She had left him for long periods; sometimes, he had asked her to go. When she came back, she knew it was to share him with others. She tried to accept this, for her love for him was as genuine as it was obsessive and possessive. But this did not make for a peaceful atmosphere. So with other women Dreiser had become very wary. He held out no false promises, no plans for the future. The immediate creation of beauty around a woman held her and upheld her in a poetry of the moment. This was also the reason for his increasing discretion and love of secrecy.

There is a section of Dreiser's *Notes on Life* called "The Necessity for Secrecy" and in it he shows how nature is full of secrets, protecting one animal from another, and often hiding her own purposes. He describes the strange leaf butterflies which have no color on one side, though they are brightly colored in flight. Wings folded, they look like dead leaves, and so escape their enemies. Another note declares:

> Life is secret, nearly entirely so, in all its phases. Nature reveals her secrets to no man, save grudgingly and peradventure. Why is this so? Because it is a fighting world, each pitted against the other. Revelation would mean death, defeat—secrecy means preservation. We cherish our own secrets and try to find out those of others.[51]

So it seemed natural to Dreiser to be secretive about his own life, his comings and his goings, about his friends, especially about women. This sometimes comes out in his letters to me, where he knew I understood his various friendships. But he did not want one woman to crowd out another. Our chief reason for concealing what we do in life is because our actions are not always logical or understandable. Easier to conceal than to explain. We do not like to be criticized or to be blamed. As the French say, *Blamer, c'est ne pas comprendre*—"To blame is not to understand."

Be that as it may, it was not easy to understand—nor to be—a person like Dreiser, with a great temperament, a hunger stronger than most mortals'; not only for sex, but for life—for living fully in the moment. How many times he was hurt, disappointed, disillusioned, gave up the chase before it was over, no one knows. No one could follow him around. Perhaps there were not as many women in his life as his critics imagine; perhaps many more. A woman has seldom spoken out against him. On the contrary, most women who knew his love, locked up the secret and the memory, with joy. And he continued to go on his devious ways, often with a great sense of solitude.

My purpose is not to judge Dreiser, nor to condone his varietism or polygamous way of life. This life, in fact, often carries its own punishment or reproach, as Dreiser wrote to me in that revealing letter quoted earlier about tearing nostalgias and vomits of agony. Some twelve years had now passed since he had written that letter. How many women, how many pangs of nostalgia had harrowed him as he worked on and tried to find peace, yet knew it could not be found? The work must come first, but hand in hand, there must be another motivation, too, a joy in living, a tenderness, a freshness. So I could not help being glad when on this first visit to New York, he told me more about the new friend, Elizabeth, he had found in California. He had described her small, Spanish-type house, where she played an Irish harp, singing folksongs, or Latin love-verses. She had a delicate face which showed through the strings of the harp as she played, dark hair, and a gentle manner. She was helping him with his work, and it was easy to perceive that she also gave him that sense of romance, of woman, that very subtle force which often parallels the great drives of life. A drive that might take the form of man to a woman, faun, lover, master—and to a man, the form of muse, mistress—even the Blessed Virgin.

This was the element which Dreiser always needed and sought, even though he knew it was fleeting. For this love magnetism must be ever renewed, refreshed, so that it did not fade out or become blocked by static emotions, but could flow freely with the stream of creation, between relationships, between women, having the illusive concept of woman—the eternal feminine—always ahead.

For all her jealousy, Helen had a full realization of this which she expresses in her book *My Life With Dreiser.* Most surprising is her dedication, on the front page: "To the unknown women in the life of Theodore Dreiser, who devoted themselves unselfishly to the beauty of his intellect and its artistic unfoldment."

Perhaps some of them were unknown, but many were highly visible, including Helen herself. How unselfish they were can also be questioned, because for all the hurt, I believe that some of them got as much as they gave. Including the satisfaction of knowing that their influence and love had entered the main stream of Dreiser's own creative action and art, enriching them, modifying them perhaps in some small degree, but blending only in a secondary way with that tumultuous current of opinion which seemed to be his birthright and which kept moving on, in spite of critics and misunderstandings. Indeed, it still moves toward its final place in the story of world literature.

Many love letters, to and from the great novelist, may surface in the years to come. Some are in the files of Dreiser's collected papers, and others, I am sure, are still treasured in private desks or attics. They are all part of his bequest of love.

Dreiser gave each woman her full value and even formed or sculptured relationships so that they were enhanced through his appreciation. Each love was different according to his woman partner, and I had the feeling that Dreiser's special gift of varying his approach was used to bring out, in each soul or personality, its own flavor. He did not wish to dominate or overpower a woman, so that she could not be her true self with him, and so feel intimidated or unable to confide in him. He loved confessions and was ready to give his compassion and understanding to any woman who opened her heart to him, whether this was accompanied by a physical surrender, or not. This is what made him a friend, as well as a lover and even a doctor of souls.

I cannot speak for others, but for me, Dreiser's friendship was a constant creative source of strength and joy. I can think of no better way to express my gratitude than to share his letters to me. They reflect our working relationship, the almost impersonal quality of our understanding and sense of life, and the flux of emotions, parallel to the passage of events. They also give me a certain right to speak for him.

I would show the letters in this book as a tribute to Dreiser's original way of thinking, his flashes of humor or sarcasm, his deep, enduring friendship, his affectionate concern and generosity that encouraged me, as it had many others, to work and write and act as I did. Or was it only our mutual destiny, as Dreiser seemed to believe, which had brought us together and put us to work, at these widely separated crossroads of our lives?

There is a great beauty of language in some of these letters: the lyric style of which Dreiser was master, when he wanted to be, and which so few critics have considered or found, among his more ponderous expressions. They are both poetic and realistic, showing deep concern for others and revealing much of his own grave and sensitive nature.

This book is about Dreiser, yet it is inevitable that I should show myself beside him, as in a photograph, to illustrate the almost wordless quality of our closeness. A few of my own letters are included to express the attraction and devotion that I felt for him.

After Dreiser had left New York, I was plunged into a mood of discouragement.[52] At that time, I did not dream of seeing him soon again, and certainly I was not jealous of the women in his life. I was like him in temperament and independence. Yet no man could take his place. I was more and more disillusioned about my work with the magazine, falling deeper and deeper into debt. I had a crazy way of rushing ahead without consulting the other editors, who were supposed to help me. But they were all busy. Partly from fear of bothering them and partly from my own stubbornness or recklessness I felt driven. By what force? Political anger? Egotism or insane optimism?

Dark clouds of war hung over everything.

Over the war years, I sometimes wrote to Dreiser, as an emotional relief for myself and because I knew he liked to get letters from women. I have never had the time to keep a diary, but sometimes, in writing to very close friends, or at a time of crisis, I have put a carbon in the typewriter to keep for the record, as a page of a journal I might someday write. I sent other letters to Dreiser, and little notes, sometimes of a practical or business nature. I do not believe he kept any of them. But a few of my carbons have survived and express perhaps better than I could now, the emotions of the moment, and that peculiar quality of our relationship that made it so consoling to be able to address him—and perhaps for him to address me. This is a typical fragment of a letter, which I had torn and then decided to keep the upper half:

November 8, 1942

Darling Teddy:

So many times I have the desire to write to you, always when I get lowest in mood or full of some sudden joy—and I never do it, because of the many killing details of life. Then, when I did write, it was to ask a favor. . . .

I hope you get this at a moment when I do not seem too remote to you, or the memory of me not too far away from your life consciousness. Strangely enough, you are always at the bottom of mine—and yet not strangely at all, because you are one of the very few great people I have been lucky enough to know—and I don't mean great in a pompous sense, but because you are one of the few rock-bottom people who lives in all the underlying truth and sadness and beauty that there is, that we can glimpse or grab.

So now, as I was trying to get some "literary" work done in the precious hours of Sunday, I heard the Brahms Piano Concerto pouring out of the radio and one of those intense moments seized me by the throat. You were suddenly very real to me.

Suddenly . . . [53]

The only other carbon I have from that period, was written almost a year later. The theme at the beginning was much the same; it was that identification of Dreiser with the deeps of music, religion, life itself. It also reflects the thoughts of a Rosacrucian ambulance driver, with whom I did volunteer work in our local hospital. On Sundays, as we sat waiting for emergencies, he would speak of this ancient form of faith which delved into psychic laws—Dreiser loved such speculations:

December 23, 1943

Dear Teddy:

Remember me? It's so long since I've written you or heard from you that silence seems more natural than words between us. And in any silence that is deep enough you are always there, Teddy, strangely at the bottom of all things. . . . That's why I've often started to write you, when some special (rare) happiness seizes me. I'm trying to attain a new severity. I don't know just what is happening to me. Something. Sometimes, I long to see you so much that I would gladly ride the rails to California. How I'd love to do it, with my son, for a change. I've been working most of the time for the last two years, first in publishing, then in a factory, then in publicity. Interesting. All very interesting. Now

I'm back with Mother again, the old place in the pines. Working one day a week in a hospital emergency room, writing and running the house, and so many things. So many things and so little accomplished. Is it always that way in life?

This is the season when the world is full of the psychic vibrations of the Christ-Spirit. A time of great power, of strong currents to be tapped, according to the Astrologists—Because of some juxtaposition of the Christ-Spirit and the sun, as some spiritual compensation for the absence of the Sunlight and coming nearer. His vibrations are strongest from the 21 of December until Christmas Eve, as they were 1943 years ago, when he was born as a man. (After Christmas, the Spirit goes down into the earth's center, where It stays during the sleep of nature rising again toward spring and coming out at the surface at Easter time, then to begin Its return to the Sun, which is consummated at the Summer Solstice? . . . Beautiful idea for the Nordic countries like Connecticut, but what happens in Australia down-under?)

But who am I to doubt any Ideas? My faith has rather grown stronger with the years. My faith in the eventual coordination of all knowledge and beauty in the bending of the knee. All this in the acceptance of tragedy and the principle of service to others. And in Love—"By this, all men shall know ye are my disciples, if ye have love one for another."

These three things you have, Teddy. Give a moment of your love to this unworthy disciple of yours, and of a common Master, call Him what you will.

Three years had passed, before Dreiser came East again. We had lived through the crisis of Pearl Harbor and now the country was wholeheartedly at war against the Nazi power. I had taken a temporary war job in a factory. Then Dreiser wrote that he was coming to receive an award from the American Academy of Arts and Letters. He wanted my services while in New York, and I was overjoyed; I answered him immediately. Soon I received the following reply. Letters such as this from Dreiser could lift me up for days and still seem to give a meaning to my life. His appreciation, though undeserved, gave me a stimulation and a confidence that was more than love. Rarely this had happened, but always when I needed it most.

March 8, 1944

Marguerite Dear:

What a warm and affectionate letter. It makes me wish to use all of your time which you so generously offer. And I will if I can. The trouble is that there are several things outside of New York—Philadelphia and Baltimore, that I will have to give some time to. Also there are publisher troubles that, alas, require straightening out. I have particular literary duties on May 19th concerning which I will write you more later. Meantime, whether you know it or not you are always somewhere in my mind shining brightly as a mental and temperamental prodigy, the girl with a wild heart and a free mind—one actually driven by the Creative force of nature itself. I wish so much that I could have you as my private secretary—year in and year out. How things would move for I could dictate to you.

Love and all good wishes,

Th. D.

I'll be writing you more a little later, and seeing you still a little later.

On Dreiser's last visit to New York, in May 1944, he had many tasks to perform, not the least his acceptance of the long-delayed recognition of his work by the American Academy.[54] Describing that spring interlude we had together provides a closer look at his enigmatic character; not only his love life, but his kindness and constant care to ennoble passing moments with significance if only by a phrase, a gesture, the refrain of a song.

This was an extraordinary experience spending all of three weeks together, which set a seal on our long but fragmentary friendship. Dreiser refused to answer the phone after six o'clock, nor would he allow me to do so, though I answered it in the daytime hours as his secretary. But if he had no urgent engagements, he wanted to spend the evenings alone. Sometimes, we still had work to finish, or we would motor out to the country in the spring evening, dine quietly together, and come back early. For the first time, we shared consecutive hours of the day and night and it was a revelation to us that this could be, and that it had never been so before.

We had never expected, certainly not demanded, more than the brief encounters which were possible between tasks and meetings with other people. Now, suddenly, it seemed as though time were running out. We had been careless with a relationship that was very precious. We were tired of all our many activities, the endless duties and desires that pushed us around. Here was something like wonderful music. We did not need to talk about it, but only to slow down and listen to it. Savor it with all our senses and thank God for it, with our souls that were tired of loneliness.

Dreiser loved to hum, when he was happy or content; he could not really sing, but he had a good musical ear and would sometimes be haunted by some popular tune of the day, usually one with nostalgic words or lilt. When I first knew him he often hummed when we were driving along in the car, and one of his favorites was "Lover, Come Back to Me," and especially the words: "I remember every little thing you used to say—No wonder I'm so lonely."

Now an old folksong had completely captured his imagination. It was English or Welsh, and I wondered if he had not heard it when he was visiting John Cowper Powys in Wales. Marian Powys was famous for her love and knowledge of folksongs, and may have been singing this one in front of the peat fire in the couple's small, stone cottage. Dreiser loved to sit in his armchair, and hum that particular song, until his mood of tenderness was complete:

O Roven, Doven, Dary O Dey
Dary O Dey
Dary O Dey
O Roven, Doven, Dary O Dey
I could not find my baby O

I found the trail of the mountain mist
mountain mist
mountain mist
I found the trail of the mountain mist
But I could not find my baby O

I found the track of the yellow fawn
yellow fawn
yellow fawn
I found the track of the yellow fawn
But I could not find my baby O
O Roven, Doven, Dary O Dey. . . .

Again those teasing, wistful repetitions typical of folksongs and which he loved as the sighing of wind, or the lapping of wavelets.

Dreiser was always the artist in his approach to women; even though his emotion might become compelling, he controlled it like a man riding a spirited horse. He was like an old centaur from Greek mythology who did not forget the laws of harmony, proportion, the desire to create poetry rather than the quick satisfaction of lust. His partner, for the moment, was possessed of all delectable qualities in his mind. He might call her name or mumble loving words and so she was raised into the mood of love, drawn into a fast-moving current of sensual feeling which varied according to circumstances. There was complete understanding, even in matters of timing. If there was a whole evening ahead of us, it would be differently spaced, emotionally speaking, than some of those fleeting hours when everything was compressed into an urgent passion.

Sometimes, in the middle of work, we would feel a closeness that demanded expression. There was a basic quality to our need, as peasants working in a field might suddenly stop and lie down together on the ground and afterwards go on working until the setting sun. They might, without realizing it, have reached a perfect unity with each other and with the land. So it would seem to us, at times, as if we had found, in the midst of complicated lives, a sudden release from all care, in an utterly simple act of love.

Now, at last, we had time to enjoy our full relationship. Hours such as Dreiser could produce, emotional beauty with passion, with tenderness, with reverence, with gratitude, with an illusion of the uttermost limits of love. How and Why? These were the questions that Dreiser was always asking as he brooded over the phenomena of science and of human living. We know something of the How: The laws of nature. In this case, how did Dreiser become such a good lover? Strength, imagination, tenderness, synchronization, bodily harmony, as that which makes a couple dance well together. But Why? Perhaps because the unleashed power of sex is intended not only to create new life—as it certainly is, in all its seriousness—but also to emulate the very contact with the Creative Force itself. Two people reaching out for the illusion, and who can say that it is not also sometimes the reality of union with some ultimate vibration, a pulsing of the very life of the universe.

What I am trying to express is much more than physical love or the ecstasy which lovers can achieve through physical or mechanical means. Not alone the thrill of a very personal or possessive love reaching its moments of fulfillment. But rather an over-love, which is so often scorned, if not altogether ignored, in the debasement and vulgarization of sex forces today.

To reach this kind of over-passion, there must be an element of love, personal or even impersonal, that ennobles, that has in it respect for life, an element of suffering, having behind it many disappointments, aspirations unfulfilled, long-waiting, all the things that make living a difficult art and love an elusive spirit. A will-o'-the-wisp, hiding behind the trees of circumstance. A psychic longing for the beauty of the past, lost and beckoning ahead, wanting to be found again. All this seemed to be implied in Dreiser's love of woman. She, too, must be made to sense these undertones and overtones, to feel the urgency of wanting something more than bodily joy. He wanted to be loved and also to create a love which, through physical unity, could approach or even touch the current of Divine Energy. That is why he was such a creative lover, one whom a woman could not easily forget.

*

Toward the end of those three weeks, the idea of continuing to work together seemed inevitable. Dreiser asked me to come to California. He had no regular secretary but called a Hollywood agency to send someone over, if he needed to type or dictate something special. In the meantime, Helen helped him. Things were not going well with *The Bulwark*. "If you come out, I think I could do it," he insisted. I could not bear to think of Dreiser not having a secretary who understood his special, totally committed way of working. But I was afraid Helen would not like it, although she had never been a literary assistant to him, and had enough to do, with the chores of being a housekeeper and a hostess. I did not want to risk any disharmony; I found myself promising to come to California at the end of the summer if Helen wrote to me that she approved and if he, too, assured me that he still wanted me to come, after he had settled back once more into the habits of his life there.

In a few weeks, Helen wrote a very cordial letter. She said that Dreiser knew he could work with me, and that he hoped to finish *The Bulwark* by spring. Then Dreiser followed Helen's letter with several of his own. I used two extracts from these letters in my former book, but here they are in their curious entirety. Not love letters—our relationship was rather an affinity, perhaps predestined? For I wonder how it was that the thin threads of circumstance that had brought us together from time to time had never been completely broken.

At the very time that Dreiser wrote me the first, almost rambling, yet intensely emotional letter, he was on the train traveling to Portland where he met Helen, and they went through the secret wedding ceremony which she describes in her book.[55] Strangely enough, he never told anyone about it, even a year afterwards. People in Hollywood had accepted Helen as his companion or common-law wife, as they had in New York, without formal inquiry, and now nothing seemed changed. Neither his biographer, Robert Elias, who came to interview him, nor his closest friends were told.[56] It was only when Helen's attitude changed toward me and toward others, as she tried to take over his life completely, that this marriage became known—and gave her some justification.[57] Looking again at the letters that follow, it is hard to understand why Dreiser did not seem to feel sure of me. I had written him a rather cool, practical letter hoping he would share it with Helen, and that he would also write me a businesslike answer which I could show to my family and others—alas, he understood my tone entirely! And his answers did not help me solve certain personal problems of my own. This unfinished letter from Dreiser in Portland began our discussion of the proposed move to California:

June 10, 1944

Here's a letter I started but couldn't finish.

Marguerite Dear: This is Thursday—And I'll be back in Los Angeles Monday and looking for a letter from you. As I wrote you I feel so keenly about you and the few days we were together—those busy, affectionate days. And I am still confronted by *The Bulwark* and the book of philosophy. Also by the, to me, so desirable and enticing thought of working toward the completion of both with and through you. For all the details of each book are so clear in my mind that I could easily outline the successive chapters or structure and once that was done paint in the various scenes—their respective colors and emotional qualities. For with you—your sensitive response to the realities and unrealities to address all would come to me clearly enough. In fact with our correlative senses of proportion I can clearly see all turgidity,—verbal as well as dramatic eliminated . . .

(This was written on a small lined memo-pad and unfinished, as Dreiser says above. It was included in a longer letter dated June 12th, which follows.)

June 12, 1944

Dearest,—Here I am at or very near Portland and getting ready to travel on to Los Angeles. But feeling *well you can guess how,* for I miss you intensely! In fact, the long slow trip, that 15-car train crowded with soldiers their wives or girls,—their noise and blether [sic] plus drinking, was enough to drive me mad. For mentally and emotionally I was seeking to be back with you in the Commodore—seeking to realize myself as there with you and yet because of the noise and clatter and marching to and fro of soldiers missing the dynamic, consoling and healing and affectionate force of you! (Lord! Lord! How am I to make out now? I'm so truly lonely.) And on the way here I have been and am worrying over how soon you will learn to do without me and how badly off I will be and am without your affectionate care and energy! Oh, you! For how none [sic] dynamic I am I never came to realized [sic] until after those first days with you—How mentally and affectionately as well as sensually a real creative personality such as yours could be and how much it could come to mean to one like myself who is slipping so thoughtlessly into the closing years. It was—while I was there with you—as though I had doubled my strength and energy & thought in fact as though you in your enduring youth had completely blended with me to produce a new youth in me,—a renewed personality. Yet here I am now! And you are gone. And I again, so lowered in strength and mood that I can scarcely present to you all of the moving things I think and feel concerning you, or us—for one thing the deep import of your natural creative energy as you transferred that to me—even, at last your to me lovely thought of coming out here to *be* with and *work with* me, for such length of time as would bring to conclusion the several things I need to do. To me as I feel about you now—after those three lovely weeks it could be forever, if you would and if there is any such thing as forever. For now, dearest, I miss you as I would a part of myself,—as if in some strange way in the past you had come to be separated from me and only now had returned into my consciousness and so myself. Only now and alas! You have vanished again. For you are not here and I feel this so great need of you. How great I wonder will you ever know? for *it is very great*.

Dearest, I may seem to be writing or talking as one in a dream—and in a way it may be that I am,—but truly, to myself, it is not so. Rather, as I have said above, it is more like a delayed revelation of fact. Something that I should have known or should have had long, long ago. And yet did not until you came to me there in New York.—Do you sense how I feel? It is not well with me just now dear, I am too too sad. But love to you,—sweet, I wish I might see you soon. Oh how I wish it!

D-

Four days later, he wrote again from the Congress Hotel in Portland:

June 16, 1944

Marguerite:
How are you dear? Do you miss me? I miss you so painfully. You may not guess how much.—Are you coming out to work with me? We could be—and would be—so creative together. I think of a hundred things to do. For myself—tired as I am—I would love to pack my bag and return. I even think of renting a room of you at your country place! All was so well with me when I was with you. And now! And now—I cannot tell you—I merely dream how it would be. Write me. And think of me. I need—*so much* of all that you have to give and care for you so deeply.

D

And again three days later from Portland:

June 19, 1944

Marguerite Dear, where are you? I arrived today from Portland—tired, very, and hoping to find a letter from you but not a word. And I have written you several times! The reason I did was because I was missing you so intensely—every day and hour on the terrible trains. And hoping you would talk more when you did of coming out here. I so wish you would. If it is a matter of money I can help you there, I think, seeing that so many agents want things now, and with you working with me I could supply them. And incidentally finish the book which I so much need to do! [*The Bulwark*] Won't you write me? Every minute, it seems, my thoughts return to you and the Commodore, for I find myself caring so much. Oh Lord! Those blissful days with you always at hand to love and talk and play with. And now! Oh, Babe do write me. Tell me about coming here. I am so emotionally miserable now. I can't tell you. I may get myself in hand but I don't want to. I only want more of those exquisite hours. Write Baby, Do.

T. D.

I wrote him as soon as I could, feeling that he was misunderstanding my silence:

June 22, 1944

Dear Teddy:

I haven't written because of the little details of life that have been buzzing around me like a swarm of bees, ever since you left. And then, there is so much to say that the time and mood are lacking to do justice to the deep as well as practical thoughts that go out in your direction, silently each day.

Nor do I want to write in an emotional vein. You speak of my coming out to work with you. We spoke of it when we were working together in New York, as we have done at various times, for fifteen years.

It is a very practical matter and one that we must decide without too much of the natural emotion which pulls us together, and also pulls us to others, because we are emotional people. . . . But Teddy, you know from our recent talks together that I have changed quite a bit in some ways and I don't think I should make the long trip and change both Hilary's life and mine, except for one reason—If you are really sure that you feel like working and finishing your novel, primarily, and that we will plan to get it done in six or eight months time—which is about the longest I should be away from Mother, and my responsibilities here. Another thing, is the matter of money, which I know you will help me with if I get stuck. I have debts all over the place because of the constant drain of the magazine, but I am used to sliding along, as it were. . . .

But most important of all, Teddy, is to be sure you really need me for the work and that Helen thinks it is a good idea. I would not want to do anything without consulting her and so I am also writing her tonight. . . . When I hear from you both, I can decide. It would not take more than about a month to pull up stakes here. If you and Helen think I should come, do write me a letter that I can show my uncle who handles my mother's affairs, so that he will understand that I'm not just going off on a lark. . . . And now I will say good-night and forgive me if I sound too businesslike. I am only disciplining myself, trying to distill the "Mountain mist, O Yellow Faun!"

This was the letter that seemed to anger Dreiser. Then came the expected letter from Helen, welcoming me to California, should I decide to come. The next day Dreiser's angry message arrived:

June 27, 1944

Dear Marguerite:

Your letter—the one and only, is such a practical and in its way dictatorial document that I hesitate to comment on it. Plainly when you simulate or endure affection in any form you are doing so for practical reasons and wish the illusion dispelled as quickly as possible lest it interfere with other emotions [to] follow. However I am not quarreling. I would like to finish the book and if your presence here with me will accomplish that I can certainly suppress any irritating emotions that may arise in me and your nonworking hours will be as free as the air.

However, there are a number of things to be taken into consideration, for now and for some time past living quarters here in L.A.—small or large are difficult to secure and are not inexpensive. Helen who has read your letter to her and approves of the idea of us working together is of the opinion that you will be lucky to secure a three-room and bath place for $35 or $40 a month. But in addition to that location—convenience of location is so important. For here distances are so great and most everyone one knows is, as a rule, some 18 to 20 miles away, studios and all. Such being the case if one does not wish to be confined to a limited and inconvenient area or neighborhood the possession of a car of some sort is really imperative. And to that must be added the fact that gas is sharply rationed. So, to enable you to live and work in comfort it may be that temporarily—until the Kisco property is sold I may not be able to undertake this joint labor much as I would like to.

Interestingly enough, Helen is all for it since she feels that the work is so necessary. Yesterday she suggested that if you cared to come and study the scene for yourself she would be glad to use her car and herself as pilot in order that you might see neighborhoods for yourself and find a place to suit you. In connection with that, I am ready to mail you a money order large enough to cover your railroad expenses to and fro. Also your room rent in some hotel pending your decision as to what you might wish to do. The reason for this last is that there are only 2 bedrooms in this house and each has his own room and bed. The way I figure is this—that once here and you care to stay and work you could decide how much you must have per week to work and live. If I can meet that—well and good I will. If I cannot you have your return fare and expenses in hand and can return no hard feelings either way. And, of course, should I not work or behave to suit you, you could always depart. Incidentally I want to apologize for mistaking what was apparently a passing practical adventure on your part for emotion and feeling. I must have seemed a dunce. But even dunces and clever practical people can make good working teams at times. Let me know how you feel about this. If you wish [to] try this program I will send on the money order.

T. D.

After Dreiser's letter of reproach, I sent a quick note on memo paper, not dated.

O Teddy Darling. . . . How can I tell you how full my heart is with thoughts of you, which you do not see, which I do not want to trust to words! You know how bitterly I have suffered because of emotional storms—and in that way, I am much older than you—Now I want things that are built upon the rock of truth and spiritual love—and not upon the sands of passions . . .

That is why I write to you, practically, of practical things, not dreaming that you would not see between the lines. . . . For what other person on earth would

I prepare to change my life, and trek across the continent? For what other man? For what other thing, but to work for the man who has meant more to me than any other in my whole life—(except my Father, these twenty-four years dead.)

To work for the man I love, because his work is the heightening of life itself, because his words and his touch are the magic of life incarnate—so that there is no line between work and love and life, in that relationship. . . .

O Teddy, write me quickly that you understand, and kiss me. . . .

Then this reply from the King's Road house:

July 5, 1944

Marguerite Dear:

Your letter of July One arrived this A.M.—So different to June 22nd with its school-marmish instructions as to what was expected as to conduct—on my part but without at least one kindly reference as to your own emotional extensions. Naturally that riled me not a little since I did not start this collaboration program. It grew out of instructions on your part as to what I was must to [sic] to extricate myself from my present literary dilemma—literary and to a degree financial. And sound enough, seeing how pervasive and mentally stimulating as well as physically arousing (and I am not referring to sex but to labor energy) is your personality—apparently from year in to year out. You are a force—a social and intellectual one and that you should find an emotional out in a seemingly endless procession of men is understandable enough. That you should begin to catechise and instruct me as to my emotional conduct for the relatively short period in which you plan to work with me—well, as you see that is another story. You struck the wrong note at the wrong time. For that I am drawn to you needs no comment at this time and unless you are drawn to me sensually as well as mentally your letters and various contacts with me over the years were masterpieces of acting and lying—(even your last six letters to me here)—to say nothing of your general approach to me in New York.

However that particular aspect of our relationship past and recent, need not be quarreled over. I took it that you were drawn to me and that if we decided to try to work together on *The Bulwark* it would not necessarily follow that a Trappistic self-restraint on my part should reign, seeing that I know full well that no such program governs in your case or ever has. Besides if the work progressed satisfactorily and you still felt this need of restraint on my part I could go elsewhere and you could go your way. Only I also know that any such schoolroom governance on the part of either would develop an atmosphere in which neither of us would be willing to work. A creative atmosphere is one in which the emotions thrive even if one works alone. And without the charm that an intellectual and emotional atmosphere usually and beautifully provides I doubt if such work as I plan could be successfully formulated. *So.*

At that (all these things said) I find you one of the most attractive and esthetically stimulating beings I have ever known. It is not a little sad—and I felt it after we first met—that you were not sufficiently drawn to me—(literary fame apart)—as to have pulled us into an esthetic and creative union. As it was you were so driven by your own desires as to be compelled to continuously explore all phases of the sex act—almost to the exclusion of the literary creative act. And so.—

Well, here we are—80 years older—and the act still dominant. You have done something with *Direction* only I so often think that with your exploring mind—not body entirely—what arresting tales—what revealing emotions you might have set forth for the world to see. However you are still young and the embodiment of electric force—*So*.

In connection with the trip you are planning I am enclosing money orders for $200. When you get here I will help you with your search (for a place to live) or Helen will and we will talk over finances. If it does not become too expensive for me we can work this thing out. And I love you as much as ever.

Th. D.

Nine days later Dreiser wrote again:

July 14, 1944

Dear Marguerite:

What has become of you?

I wrote you a long letter enclosing two money orders for $100.00 each. And have been expecting to hear that they reached you. Also to feel myself worthy of another affectionate letter. That last one cheered me no little for the time being. It was like the best of our days at the Commodore and that's not hinting that they weren't all lovely to me—work or no work. The one thing that I resented most was the constant stream of callers and telephone messages. It was wearing and worse, keeping me away from you or you from me. For never in my life before did I ever have anyone who managed so completely and thoughtfully and so brought things to as successful ending as they could have been brought. Also the super intelligence and harmony that went with it all. I could think of nothing but praise and did not while with you. Now that I think it all over I marvel that *Direction* has not been built up into a nationally welcome and consulted sociologic and esthetic guide book. For you certainly have the mental and esthetic material with which to build it. Also I can see you as a story writer—an interpretive and moving one. Where hast thou been Oh searchlight? And where are the pictures of living that you must have observed. You recite so many tales and present so deftly so many characters!

Well Sweet do you know that I am lonely for you? Or don't you want to know? The days here after my weeks with you not only seem but *are dull* and trying. For alas, I temperamentally hold an angle on life that requires a correlative one. And that I have not, for you are not with me and worse you may not want to be. But Oh, how I would like trying this proposed period with you even though you did not—eventually—consider it successful, for I think it would be. For there is that about you that stirs me to action even though I may only be retracing certain hours and discussions that involved us both. For one thing I think I could dictate certain short stories that I am sure would come out better for the mere telling of them to you. And so, Lady Adventure, I look forward to

> the hours when we will be trying these out and deciding what we shall decide. Curiously, as much as I would like to dwell on the stirring affection for you that I have there was something about that first instructive letter of yours that chilled and angered me. It seemed so like a sharp and in part repressed! criticism of the entire period we were together and that seemed a little too much—as though I had failed to sense a concealed attitude which had involved dissatisfaction on your part and worse a phase of reproach which was then—at long last being allowed to manifest itself. Oh me! Oh my!—Well and however all that is now past and done for. I have put it all aside. Your charming love letter did that and now I only wish that I might see you—feel the mental and at times emotional brightness of the days you so easily make. And that banishes—in part—the dullness of waiting, for you do not know I am sure with what desire—what sense of impending work and achievement I look forward to these coming months of work backed by the inspiration and affection. It drives away grayness and lonliness [*sic*] for me. As for you sweet? ?
>
> D

Finally everything was arranged; my son was as eager to go to school in Hollywood, and to see California, as I was. We packed up our old car, planning to stop only at Dreiser's birthplace in Terre Haute and for a brief visit to the Grand Canyon. It was with high spirits that we started off on our first long trip across the country.

The last period of my work with Dreiser was a singular experience of harmony and accomplishment, a high plateau of companionship and effort. It brought to fruition Dreiser's unique novel, *The Bulwark.* Started before 1915, put aside and done partially in several versions, it represents a long development in Dreiser's thinking and a final, mystical understanding of the universe, focusing the insights revealed in his *Notes on Life.* Places were always important to Dreiser's work, and he must have the proper setting if he were to attain that creative concentration he craved and had so seldom been able to find because of the many cross-purposes and conflicts in his life.

It was wartime and very difficult to find apartments in Hollywood, as Helen had predicted. I stayed at a motel, cut into the hillside above Cahuenga Passa—a lovely spot, surrounded by palmettos and tall oleanders, on the way to the San Fernando Valley. You could see mountains in the distance, and the graceful peak of Cahuenga, nearby. My son enrolled in the Hollywood High School and Dreiser said he wanted to begin work at once. He lived only a short distance away. I was to pick him up every morning as he preferred to work in a place away from the clutter of his own desk. He had worked so at Mount Kisco in one of the cabins, seldom in the big house.

That first day, Dreiser had with him only a manila envelope and his book, *Twelve Men*.[58] He said he could not begin to bring the boxes of material relating to *The Bulwark* until I had a permanent apartment. I determined then to find a place in this neighborhood where there would be beauty and quiet. I will never forget those first days of the mild, California climate, flowers everywhere, the new landscape stretching away and the happy anticipation of the work ahead.

Dreiser had brought his old story, "Culhane, the Solid Man" from his book, *Twelve Men,* and wanted to add humorous details which he remembered from his stay at a health resort to which his brother Paul had sent him, years before, to save him from a grave depression and almost suicidal mood. He had recently sold a script of Paul's life, entitled *My Gal Sal,* to the Hollywood tycoons, and was sure that Culhane's life could also make a saleable and lively script. He proceeded to dictate some amusing and scandalous scenes concerning Culhane's French housekeeper, who was his secret love. Culhane, whose name was really Muldoon, ran a luxury health establishment which attracted many rich men with drinking problems. He tried to maintain a very strict and almost bullying attitude toward his clients, but many things happened behind his back. Dreiser was sure that a riotous comedy could be made of this sobering-up process in some of its lighter aspects.[59] One did not easily think of Dreiser as a humorist, yet sometimes he could roar with laughter and glee over a ridiculous paradox of human behavior, and a good case could be made for his writing of comic episodes, throughout his career. Perhaps it was to counteract the sense of tragedy that often weighed on him, and the irony he felt about the inequities of the social system. In his *Notes on Life,* he had a section on humor, examining its source, which is usually based on exaggeration and direct or indirect cruelty.

But that day, as he laughed, another mood came over him. The papers slipped from his hand. "Come, sit by me," he murmured in his lowest, most vibrant voice. Then he pressed me against his white, linen coat. Below his white hair and dark brows, his gaze bore down on me. Outside, masses of white oleanders wafted their fragrance through the half-closed venetian blinds. A moment in time.

My son, by chance, exploring the paths and steps above our motel, found a tiny house, with a patio sculptured into the hillside. We persuaded the owner to let us rent it unfurnished, although he wanted to sell it. We promised to move out if it were sold. We had very little money for furniture, but procured two beds, a long table and two wicker chairs, one of them a rocker for Dreiser. He liked the motion of rocking ever so slightly, to calm the restlessness of his nerves. And he loved the bareness of my new place, the uncluttered living room, opening on to the patio on one side, and on the other, high enough above the ground to give a view of the distant San Gabriel Mountains.[60]

Here he began to bring his precious bundles of *The Bulwark* manuscript. After several weeks of sorting and making outlines of the material previously typed, we were ready to begin the new task of putting together everything that was to be used. By Christmastime, Dreiser was able to undertake the writing of the last third of his story, since the first two-thirds had already been done, in three different versions. Because the detailed story of the material as it shaped up at this time has been given in my former book, I will dwell here only on the psychological atmosphere in which the work was completed.[61]

Dreiser had, of course, many friends in Hollywood, but now he was determined to see none of them until he had finished *The Bulwark*. I also knew a few people there, a writer in particular whom I was supposed to look up, but Dreiser begged me not to do this. "I don't want people knowing about my work—I don't want you running around with all sorts of friends while this is going on," he said, gruffly. At first, I was a bit surprised at this attitude, but then I realized that all my life I had been distracted by many persons and many activities and so had never accomplished the writing I had hoped to do. Dreiser was right. Creative work must be a way of life. For his part, he told Helen not to accept any invitations nor to give any parties during the next months. Helen knew that he meant it, when he retired into a working mood. But Dreiser was adamant in expecting me, too, to concentrate on him and his work.

Our day was centered around the hours he worked in the little house, from about ten until four, when I took him home, and did the few errands necessary to my simple housekeeping. Then I was joined by my son, coming home from school. For the most part, we spent evenings at home, he with his homework, and I returned to Dreiser's papers again. Truly, there was no time when they were out of my mind. And Dreiser, too, would frequently tell me of some thought he had had during the night. Some mornings he had a few penciled pages for me to copy.

Once or twice a week, Dreiser and Helen took us out to dinner. Helen loved to drive and did not care much for cooking. So we would motor out to the country, or along the shore for a simple meal, and return early. These were pleasant hours and we all enjoyed views of land and sea. Sometimes, Dreiser wanted me to drive him out alone, and this I would not do. I respected Helen's right to be with him in the evenings, as I wished to be with my son. So we avoided all conflict.

Helen was happy and grateful that we were getting along well with *The Bulwark,* because Dreiser and she needed the income from a new book. Their funds were very low. Helen said they could only pay me $25 a week, but I was to get ten percent of the profits, after the book was published. This was written out in the form of a letter signed by Dreiser. I did get four hundred dollars as my share of the new advance Dreiser received from Doubleday. This helped to get a few more essentials for the little house I had recklessly rented unfurnished. But I was glad that Helen had warned me of the wartime scarcity of apartments and that I had crossed the country in my old car, which was indispensable to us now.

Gradually we settled down to the work of finishing *The Bulwark.* For the first weeks Dreiser brought new boxes and envelopes filled with his earlier scripts. Almost every day until finally we had them all sorted out and prepared to go on. Only occasionally, a mood of deep emotion would break into our working hours. Between the pages of my first manuscript about Dreiser, written during the months after his death, I found this page, not used, a reaction to some day of emotion too strong to describe. It paints a mood of which I do not even remember the details. I let it stand as a picture without a place or a frame:

> That day, September 26, we were still so saturated with emotion that we could hardly speak to each other when we met. I came in T.'s drive and saw him watering the bushes and flowers around the pool. He looked at me almost scowling. . . . Then he shut off the water and we sat down, he on the yellow bench in front of the long, garden table, and I on a garden chair. I remember that there was a new water lily which had come out in the neat little pool which was always kept fresh and filled with water from the hose. It was a pinkish-yellow lily of some striped variety. We talked a moment about the work and decided that we had better work on, each alone, that day, and that we would also do that on the following day, and I would not even phone at nine o'clock as I usually did to learn his plans. We both realized that we had reached some emotional climax the day before, which should not be touched, even by words and should not be repeated, in any form, for some time. . . . We realized that we could not work and get enough done if we often let ourselves go into these deeper emotional periods, creative as they were. For we had a way of playing on each other's nerves and feelings, telling each other also the facts of our lives, as if we were so close that it was without effort and very simple, and with mutual relief to us

> both, we spoke about our former relations with others who had made up the strange pattern of our lives, and about each other. How we had missed getting more closely involved when we first met.[62]

Dreiser had also talked very beautifully of Helen, in those days of the strong emotions. Saying how unique and all-of-a-piece and simple her love for him had always been. And he repeated the story, that I had heard him tell before, as he had also written about it, describing how she had built their early life in Hollywood, through her own initiative. She went from one studio to another, obtaining small parts in the silent movies, and then larger parts, and was able to meet their expenses while Dreiser stayed at home in their Glendale bungalow, writing. And when he felt he must get back to New York, she gave up her promising career to follow him. Her love for him had certainly given her life a special significance. Now, she was one of the few surviving characters of the many love-dramas in his life.

With the task of depicting a Quaker community and the crucial character of Solon Barnes in *The Bulwark,* Dreiser was openly interested in religious services. If there had been a Quaker meeting nearby, we would surely have visited it, but the nearest one was in Whittier, some sixty miles away. However, we found a Congregational church which was led by a most unusual minister. Allan Hunter offered something different; it was silent prayer, as practiced in the Quaker tradition. In his conventional Sunday-morning worship, he introduced the element of meditation. He would try to put his congregation in a state of quiet and awareness of a spiritual reality. Then he would hold a silence as long as he could until someone began to stir or cough, and the spell was broken.

This technique of Hunter's intrigued Dreiser greatly, for he held his own kind of meditation—brooding concentration on his work. He had also read much about Oriental methods of prayer and we heard that Allan conducted a meditation group on Wednesday nights, which included many who did not follow the Christian faith. Allan had also been to India and met with the great practitioner of nonviolence, Mohandas Gandhi. On a visit later, to the little house on the hillside, Allan told Dreiser much about his Indian trip. The two men had seemed completely at home with each other—enjoying the sunshine of our open patio.[63]

On this patio, much of Dreiser's creative work was done. The patio was hardly bigger than a large room. The patio's walls were those of the house on two sides, and the others were of low stones mounting into banked flower beds which, in turn, melted into the rising meadow beyond. My son and I had weeded and planted flowers in abundance, nasturtiums sprouting between the stones. Far beyond was the stretch of the San Gabriel Mountains.

Often, when Dreiser asked for the fresh typing of a page, he would take it out to a settee and small table on the patio, and brood over it, while I typed inside. He might change it, or just sit for a long time; then come in with a new, pencilled page for an entirely different section of his story. His mind often jumped ahead to some idea for an unwritten chapter. Sometimes, he wanted to discuss the writing in general. But I said very little. I had learned that he could best find his own expressions, fish out of the depths of his original mind the most unpredictable sequences of words and rhythms.

Elsewhere, I have made a long study of Dreiser's style, his inimitable way of putting words together, his long and short rhythms which came to him naturally, as his way of walking or talking. A common sport among literary critics has been to deride Dreiser's style, calling his writing undistinguished, clumsy. One of the main reasons for his apparent awkwardness is that through the years, his work was cut and altered by editors, advisors, and even his best friends, who had no ear for the illusive qualities of his prose, and were simply impatient with its slow tempo, its original language. When his long line and rhythm are not destroyed, his literary music is as unmistakable as compositions of Rachmaninoff or Shostakovich.

Dreiser never worried much about his style, though, but only about the accuracy of his descriptions. He liked to build up some statement with small, one- or two-syllable words, like bricks, placed with care and patience. Where a slick contemporary writer might use one or two examples, and pass on to another scene of action, Dreiser would sit for minutes, half an hour, over a sentence, to make sure it encompassed all he wanted to say. He would often pile up ten ways of expressing emotion in a single sentence. And looking over it, he would be more inclined to add a word or two, than to remove a brick already placed.

Another technique which he used deliberately was the connective word that, he told me, made for smoothness of style. Paragraphs begin with an "And" or a "But" or a "Yet." How many of these have been slashed out by editors as unnecessary! An endless record of changes might be noted in the Dreiser manuscripts, as well as illustrations of his best, unaltered prose. But it is especially in *The Bulwark* that we can find the long, slow rhythms intended to create a kind of largo of literary music. As, for example, the sentence which started the last chapter:

> And so, at last, the final obsequies for Solon Barnes at Thornbrough, that originally so beloved home of his father and mother; and after his father's death, of himself and Benecia; and from which, throughout the first ten years of married life at least, he had experienced nothing but spiritual joy, mingled as that had been, yet not of his own seeking, with material comfort.[64]

Almost the whole story is there, compressed into a sentence redolent of mood. A rich convolution of facts and emotions which the reader has already known and now feels again, with a deep nostalgia.

Dreiser sometimes built up a scene that could stand alone, like a painting, at the turning point of a story. So it was with the scene in *The Bulwark* where Stewart's body is brought back from the jail in which he had killed himself out of remorse. Dreiser had thought of this episode many years earlier, when first planning his novel. He wrote it out on small sheets of paper, later pasted on regular typewriter size. He wanted to see if his plot had in it the seeds of a full-length tragedy. After writing some eight pages, he felt that "this would work" (as he expressed it) and yet it took some thirty years before this scene became the core of the published novel.

One should not consider Dreiser's style alone, in following him into the reaches of his somber moods. Often, he wrote as though it were from some inner dictation, a natural flow of his deepest thought. Though he might alter and discard what was finally on paper, this was his basic, creative act, from which his way of writing and his style are inseparable. Probably every writer has his or her basic style, which is an instinctive way of thinking, of talking, letter writing as well as creative writing. The more self-conscious and polished an author's style, the less the writing resembles these other means of communication. With Dreiser, the spoken word was very close to the written, because both were the product of his desire to express the thought in him in its most exact and natural way, rather than to play, or make art with it. This is also what made dictation to another person relatively easy for him. But because he was himself, a remarkable person, his style was beautifully evocative.

Finally, we reached the end of Solon's story and there was nothing more to do but the careful checking over of each page and carbon. The almost sacred cocoon of concentration in which we had held *The Bulwark* was broken.

*

Even though it may seem to be always summertime in California, the spring does come with a different warmth and many new flowerings. The two small peach trees outside the living room had come into bloom. We remembered how they had looked in September, when their fruit hung in pink and yellow spheres, tempting us to reach out and pick them from the window. But now their blossoms had a more fragile beauty. There had also come to be a slight difference in our relationship. Perhaps we were tired, but working with this Quaker material, in the closeness of our understanding, physical emotions were not so important. They were sublimated to some extent by the kind of love that Dreiser had expressed in *The Bulwark*. Solon achieved it through nature and his Quaker faith, and then so did his daughter Etta, who had been abandoned by her lover, and had come home to console her father. Sharing his sense of the beauty of nature, she herself becomes suddenly aware of a deeper meaning, of a mystical love experience. No wonder then, that our spirits were permeated, too, by this invisible love. The last weeks of working on *The Bulwark* were filled with a peace and satisfaction for which there are no words. The manuscript was sent off to the publishers on May 3, 1945. Perhaps nothing was ever the same again. Only when the time was over, did we realize what this period had meant to us.

Ensenada, white beach in the sun, was the first place that welcomed us to a rest and change of mood. We had taken a short vacation with Helen and Hilary to this beautiful, wild seaside about two hours' ride, below the Mexican border. There were plans to develop it as a gambling resort, but then it was completely unspoiled. We swam in warm, green waves rolling in from a dreamlike tropical island several miles away. We stretched out on the very fine, white sand and chatted casually, Helen and I doing most of the talking. She was particularly glad that our work was over and that now she was free to plan a few parties and go out with Dreiser.

We were gone only a few days, but the spell of our being alone in the sanctuary of our work was definitely broken. Dreiser had no idea, however, of giving up work on other things. There were several short stories he proposed to dictate, and he wanted to come to the little house on the hill every weekday morning. I was going to stay there until my son finished school, in June, and then we had promised my aging mother to return to our country home in Connecticut.

Dreiser was not happy about this, although I had promised to come back in September if he needed me. My son liked the Hollywood High School and his excursions on the ocean with the Sea Scouts. They camped out on the beautiful island of Catalina, and sailed an old schooner. Although our house had been bought by a French couple, they were willing to continue renting it to us for another year. Why could Dreiser not let us go gladly, if he knew we were willing to return? But he did not want us to leave at all.

"No," he grumbled. "If you go, you may not come back." He seemed to imply that if we left, we would be in the hands of an inscrutable fate, and so might not be able to return. Was it his old belief in destiny, that man's will is not free? When I questioned him about this he merely retired into gloomy silence. Better not to talk about it but enjoy our last month on the hillside.

We spent more time on the patio, where the ice flowers were in their last bloom. The nasturtiums were running riot all over the stones. Dreiser started to compose an odd story, drawn from his own experience in his boardinghouse days, called "The Total Stranger."[65] It concerned a working man who hears a couple quarreling, through the flimsy wall of the next room. Finally, the man cannot resist speaking to them, telling them that he had thrown away his marriage in much the same way, and that now he was intolerably lonely. The story was typical of Dreiser's concern for the lives of quite commonplace people, with their troubles and heartaches.

We also looked through the manuscript of *The Stoic*. Dreiser said of it: "Helen wants to finish this with me, but I'm sure you could do it." Just glancing through the story outlines troubled me. "I'd rather work on the philosophical *Notes,*" I said, "if I come back."[66]

"*If* you come back," he echoed in his lowest, darkest tone. Why did he not have the confidence in my promise to return if he wanted me? He did not ask me, directly, as if it were not something that we could decide for ourselves. The whole situation puzzled me, and Helen did not make it any easier. She was vague about any future plans, and she had already drawn Dreiser into a series of social activities.

As I look back on this period, I realize that Helen did not want me to return, but she was too tactful to say so. She was simply waiting for my departure to take over Dreiser's life completely. He knew this himself, and did not want to get into any more fights with her. He believed that somehow things would work themselves out.

The Sunday night before our departure, Hilary and I planned to have supper in Olivera Street, in the Mexican quarter of Los Angeles. Dreiser and Helen had introduced us to this colorful little byway that on Sundays seemed to be in a continual state of fiesta. At the last moment, Hilary was invited elsewhere by young friends and I drove down alone.

The narrow street was crowded as usual; pulsating and tuneful music wafted out from many small restaurants and bars. While looking for a place where we had had enchiladas, I stopped at a long bar half-opened on the sidewalk. I did not often stand at a bar without a companion. Suddenly, a dreadful sense of loneliness and despair came over me. What if I never did return to Hollywood? What would I do? Start once more on the crazy search for other adventures, other men? No. I did not want to go back to my old life. Even though a cruel premonition told me I might never be so close to Dreiser again, even if I stayed in California. But I must keep this sense of climax, of beauty. There was a mirror behind the bar, and I raised my glass, drinking to my own image and to Dreiser whom I felt at my shoulder: "To my last lover."

Then another happy afternoon on the patio. We made light of our parting the next day. It didn't seem as though our companionship could ever come to an end. Time had nothing to do with it. It would not run out like the sands in an hourglass. How many years since we had first met? Almost twenty. Our attraction to each other had never changed, only developed and reached a higher point.

And so we left in good spirits, my son and I, having the prospect of a leisurely trip back across our great country, camping out in the Grand Canyon and visiting an Indian reservation which we had not had time to do on our way out.

Dreiser's next letters followed me to Connecticut, making me realize that there had been this time in California that nothing could take away. The first was written the day after we left.

> June 24, 1945
>
> So my golden girl is gone! No one to call me up at ten in the morning or arrive at that time! No one with the brisk step and engaging optomistic [*sic*] smile, and the desire to be thinking and doing—thinking of and doing some new, interesting thing. No one wishing to spread happiness even to borders of so pessimistic temperament as mine. That one (the one) who was always sure that things were for the best—one who believed that prayer—the right prayer—was always answered and should be. The liveliest and most engaging temperament that [I] have known in most of my years and the one to whom I have been most keenly drawn—I and my pessimistic temperament. And now she has gone and already at nine o'clock of this bright day I feel her going and her absence so keenly— so very keenly! And yet outside all is as before—the flowers, the grass,

the trees, the pool—all but the Golden Girl. Mentally and emotionally I can see her coming and going and yet so painfully beyond my sight let alone my reach.

O how I wish I might reach her! Look into her laughing eyes,—see her laughing smile; hear her comforting voice! And now how will I find the spirit to work. Now when I need her so much! And Darien is so far away—so very far really.

Well, my golden girl is gone! And now I can only try to wish that in some good or rather believe that in some fortunate [time] I will see her again—face to face. Oh! to me you golden shining spirit—all is *so very sad now*—so painfully gray. Will you send me some helpful word? I know one word. *Love*

D.-

And again:

July 10, 1945

Marguerite:

This isn't a love letter but it is one of regret that you are not here to move and shine with great and small your gift of interest in all things. You awake each day. You arise and look about you seeking forth with that which needs encouragement, recognition, celebration[.] Even "Whom shall I help today"—It is so that you impress me.

Dear, Hello!

Luck and strength and survival of that intense interest that I admire so much. Love and prayers for your success.

D.

Maybe you will come back in September?

And yet again:

No Date

Marguerite Dear:

I miss your stirring spirit so much—your lively inquiring mood—your energetic readiness to take life as it is—what it has to offer and always without complaint or nearly so. Since you left here two or three letters have come—one addressed directly to me. As for the other two, I chanced to see one to Helen, but her mood is such that she prefers to conceal them! I am prepared to rent a box somewhere, P O, or else, and would this week, only it looks as though both of us will have to drive to Portland in order to be there when the end arrives, if it does.

We may be gone for 3 weeks but you may write me there if you choose. The address is, c/o Hayes, *7638 East Yamhill Street,* Portland, Oregon. Only remember, letters or no letters I'll be thinking of you and missing you all the while. Incidentally, I'll have *The Stoic* to work on. Meanwhile send me kind thoughts and I'll scribble mine and send them to you. Meanwhile here is love and all good wishes. I think so much of the little house and the happy work and happy hours we spent there.

Yours,

D.

The summer was half over, yet I had received no direct summons to return to Dreiser. I missed his voice, his touch, his understanding, the feeling of taking part in a work which I knew was so much more important than any of my own literary efforts. He seemed to miss me, too, but his beautiful letters only stirred a longing to see him, without giving me practical instructions. Finally, I wrote asking him to answer quite simply whether we should plan to come, for I did not wish to make any difficulty for him.

Then I received a strange, enigmatic letter from King's Road quoting the witches from *MacBeth*. I don't know why I allowed it to be published in *The Collected Letters of Theodore Dreiser,* except that they were edited by Robert Elias, who had shown himself to be my friend, and he had requested it. The letter can be understood only in the light of what subsequently happened in California, and seems odd, out of context. When I first read it, I was as puzzled as before. There was something sinister and challenging about it. Yet it seemed that, between the lines, Dreiser was calling out to me. I felt that I must go back and stay, if only until the proofs of *The Bulwark* were done.

August 25, 1945

Double, Double, Toil and Trouble
Fire burn and cauldron bubble

D

I turn and fret and worry. I had your understanding letter days ago, but as for an agreeable Solution for you and for me?—*not so easy.* Worry, jealousy. Discord. The feeling of injustice—unfairness[.] A sense of unjustified scheming and plotting. And eventually *for some one*—retribution[.] And because of all this the difficulty of creative labor.

As for myself I have but four hundred dollars at the moment that I could devote to your coming here—the same to be charged off to twelve weeks of salary at $25.00 weekly. That more than $400 may fall into my hands before the twelve weeks have passed is entirely probable but at that not absolutely. The only trouble or problem—is that of CONTACT—our being together enough without outside irritation and friction to make the matter of constructive work—constructive writing possible.

Double, Double, Toil & Trouble
Fire burn and cauldron bubble

And yet if you were here! If you came of your own accord and were settled—had that little house or a room and a position in a movie that required only a portion of your time—rest to be devoted to us—to work—how quickly probably this dream of happy contact and serious constructive labor might be realized. I have been working steadily—not always successfully but steadily. And of course I have grieved over your absence. For mostly you carry the

> atmosphere of creation with you. You evoke effort [,] the atmosphere of creative work with you—also the happiness of creative work with you—and so. Yet even now [if] I had the ease of ample means I would send you the money and see if you would come and try to solve this. But as things are I am too disturbed [,] too distrait to urgently suggest this. It seems too inadequate—too inefficient and yet maybe not. You may be pondering all this disturbedly as I have been doing. Hence I write[.] It is perfectly clear I think. Only I hate delay—the lack of sufficient means just now to arrange all. For above all I need the aid of a practical mind that can look after and handle for me so many practical details.
>
> If you answer register your letter to me—personal delivery[.][67]

When we returned to Hollywood, the situation had indeed changed. Dreiser was not as strong, and Helen did not want him to go out, nor to do any other work. He was finishing *The Stoic,* with her assistance, and she said he did not want to be disturbed. However, when she saw that I accepted the new circumstances, she was pleasant and cordial as usual. Dreiser sent me to his agent, but since I could not find a literary job, I took an interesting assignment from the Red Cross, for which I had had some wartime training. But if I did not come to see him almost every day, Dreiser sent for me, and we went out to sit in his garden.

It was a new phase of our companionship. We talked freely but I could sense that he was afraid of displeasing Helen. He wanted me to pick him up at the corner drug store (the famous Schwabs on Sunset Strip) and drive him to the little house on the hill. But I would not do this. He assured me that other friends had met him there and Helen knew nothing about it. This I doubted, for she was very watchful. She had also taken me aside and told me that their old love relationship had bloomed afresh. I could sense this in her way of dressing, her typical short skirts and low-cut blouses. She was still a very attractive woman. That she should take advantage of her new power was only natural. Dreiser needed her help more than ever in the practical details of daily living. Yet I noticed that she was less careful about what they ate and drank; she knew how to arouse his emotional nature. She could also indulge her own high-strung jealous temperament, and he could not simply walk out, as he had so often done in the past.

In the garden he told me that he had accepted this attitude of Helen's, so that he could finish *The Stoic,* and when that was done, he hoped that in some devious way, he would be able to work again with me. Suddenly I saw the whole picture: the strange letter evoking conflict, trouble, intrigue. Certainly on the part of Helen if anyone would oppose her now. It would not be me. To fight and be jealous was not my way. If there was any reality in the "greater love" that I had touched with Dreiser, then it should be strong enough now to let us retire from the sexual arena. No one woman could have been the complete or perfect mate for Dreiser, nor do many men of genius find their female counterpart. I think of the case of Madame Curie and her husband, who were united in their common love and devotion to their work, but here, she seems to have been the genius of the two. There is also the famous couple of the Brownings, Robert and Elizabeth, but these are probably exceptions that prove the rule. Many more couples have achieved an ideal partnership on a humbler level of work and personality, struggling together or serving their children in anonymous, creative love. This element in love relationships carries persons over the inevitable disillusion with one another, or past the inevitable wearing-down of the sexual attraction of one body for another. There is an almost automatic or subconscious lessening of stimulation in relationships based on sex alone—even though they may seem to be clothed in romantic love.

Dreiser told me once of his surprise when Kirah Markham, with whom he had been having a passionate relationship for several years, suddenly said to him: "Teddy, you don't love me any more." He had hardly been conscious of the change, but when she blurted it out, he was forced to face it. She was too intelligent, too sensitive, not to sense deceit if he denied it, but he had not intended to break with her so soon, nor did he want to hurt her.

"Why, I guess I don't," he said, quite amazed at his own admission, and indeed this was the beginning of the end of a long and happy affair. How often Dreiser had experienced this changing of one stimulus for another, and how often he expressed it in his stories. Describing the artist Eugene Witla in *The 'Genius,'* Dreiser wrote how again and again his protagonist imagines himself to be hopelessly, inextricably in love despite all of his experience to the contrary. This was typical of the illusion of love deliberately embraced by Dreiser himself. It was part of the pattern of his love life.

There was another, less noble, third element—in the form of another person—in Dreiser's case. A second woman, making a triangle with him and another mistress. Dreiser being pulled in two directions by two jealous women, and finding that this gave him a sense of tension, stimulating to his creative imagination. Certainly the world of literature is full of emotional triangles in every possible and impossible combination, and this has yielded much psychological fruit.

In her very honest book, Helen describes such a triangle that had lasted many months; finally, the "other woman" had a long conversation with her on the phone. She was leaving the city, as Helen had done first, because of her, but now she admitted defeat, noting that Dreiser always came home to Helen. And Helen concludes her description of the encounter as follows:

> I learned that Dreiser had liked the stress and strain of that particular creative period so much that he attempted again and again to repeat it. He tried to place himself between opposing forces in order to gather reactions of a stimulating quality and character, and at the same time to safeguard himself against being weakened or destroyed by the indispensability of any one person.[68]

Here, there flashed through my mind that line of Oscar Wilde's from "Reading Gaol," which Dreiser felt so deeply, about each man killing the thing he loves.[69] Dreiser experienced this fear both concerning himself and those he loved. There was too much passion and too much vulnerability in his nature to enable him to escape easily from any emotional involvement, as if he felt life itself sucking him up, licking from his very bloodstream the prodigal strength that could well up or drain out, cause joy as well as despair.

Helen was also capable of extremes of emotion. But her love had entangled itself around one person, Dreiser. An early marriage and perhaps some romances that had tempted her as a charming young actress meant absolutely nothing to her, once she had found this great, dynamic lover. He became her life, and for three years they shared a happy love in the simple cottage in Hollywood, where Dreiser worked on his writing, while Helen went the round of the studios, finding small parts, and then bigger ones. She had the talent to become a star of those early, silent-movie days, as Dreiser liked to relate. But when he began to be restless and wanted to go back to New York, she did not hesitate a moment to leave all chance of a career behind.[70]

Her love had the tenacity of one who had staked her very existence on that of this man who was all force, all fascination to her. Later, when she saw that she must share him with others, the agonies and jealousies that she endured did not quench her love nor her desire, but seemed to fan the flames of a possessive love which grew with her determination to stay beside him. Then, as he finally entered a new and ever more tumultuous period of success and fame, to share it with him, at any cost. At that period, in the glamorous studio on Fifty-seventh Street, Helen described her own struggle, and how she literally fought for sanity, as she reached out for the teachings of Yoga, and went up on the roof of the huge apartment house to practice breathing and calming exercises. She then realized that she worshipped this uncontrollable lover, and that her love had become a tyranny over her very soul.

This is indeed the tragedy of lovers without that struggle together for the children that can balance and protect the naked emotions, cover raw wounds of passion and despair. The literature of the world would be poor without these unrelieved dramas, the sad, sublime poetry of love lost, or death. But the love directed and shared with a third love, love for children, for common work, or for a shared ideal, has another dimension. Helen saw this, realized it, finally, but she could not entirely live by it, and so escape the storms and torments of her own emotions. Yet who can say that she did not help Dreiser fulfill his destiny—and her own, by her very importunity, like the "importunate widow" in the Bible, whose story is told in Luke 18:25.

> There was in a city a judge, which feared not God, neither regarded man: And there was a widow in that city; and she came unto him, saying, "Avenge me of my adversary." And he would not for a while: but afterward he said within himself, "though I fear not God, nor regard man; Yet because this widow troubleth me, I will avenge her, lest by her continual coming, she weary me."

A story once made the rounds to the effect that Horace Liveright offered to put aside a sum for Helen, if she promised to leave Dreiser, and the Fifty-seventh Street studio. This was the time of the great success of *An American Tragedy,* which Liveright had brought out. The publisher was distressed by stormy scenes he had witnessed and felt that Helen, above all, wanted money. I do not think that Dreiser agreed, although Helen would say anything when she was in a rage.

Dreiser was always sensitive to Helen's suffering, even though he had always gone his own way. Again and again, she had taken him back, and managed the practical details of his daily life. And he had appreciated this, more and more, as he grew older. "She's been around a long time," he said to me in the garden once. "Look at those flowers. She put them in by the pool yesterday."

Now at last, Dreiser had determined in his inscrutable way, and probably directed by those forces that he felt guided him, to give Helen the security and devotion that she had waited for for so many years. There was great nobility in his gesture of marrying her and giving her the reward of being his widow and legal heir.[71] Deeper than gratitude. In his own mind, almost an act of justice, of reparation. To Helen, it was most of all the satisfaction of his presence and love. In her book, she describes a renewed tenderness between them. One could sense that they lived in an atmosphere of marriage that had never been so apparent before.

Whatever the peace agreement between the two of them, Dreiser's garden was a tranquil place. It answered his need for beauty in nature, and made a frame for his deepest meditations. It was an even, spacious rectangle of land, bordering fences in the background hardly noticeable behind bushes and palms. In the center of the lawn was a gracefully shaped, irregular pool, with plantings of miniature bamboo, odd grasses, and blue azuretum. Goldfish gleamed in the deep part of the water, and sometimes a small, green frog appeared.

There was a table with garden chairs to which Dreiser brought pillows from the house, arranging them with a grave courtesy, which was like his literary style, slow and harmonious when its line was not disturbed. Birds came into the branches near Dreiser, seeming to know his vibrant voice. Many nature observations were collected in those last months, scribbled in pencil and slipped into his file, as the result of his hours of musing and meditation, here, under the luscious shade of his tall avocado tree which stood near the pool. This tree he put, like a literary character, into the very original and detailed account of his thoughts on nature and its wonders that resulted in his essay of twelve pages, "My Creator," dated Hollywood, 1943. He had intended it to be published as a separate piece, a sort of declaration of belief. But it had never been accepted and it was left in his files to be published after his death.[72]

Coming home from work, I sometimes stopped in at King's Road, and if I missed several days, Dreiser would send for me. Sharing his hours in the garden was like listening to some inner music. Little conversations, affectionate words, did not interfere nor seem to make much difference in the peaceful experience of our communion with nature.

So the fall months slipped by. Winter was coming, but it had no menace in California. Then Christmas was approaching, the darkest time of the year, yet time of spiritual light. By some strange timing, the proofs of *The Bulwark* arrived, just as I was to take a short vacation with my son. Helen felt obliged to tell me this, but said that I did not need to bother about them. She would do them with Dreiser. I went down to King's Road to insist on seeing them, since Dreiser and I had worked on the book so long and with such care and concentration.

I will not repeat the whole scene between Helen and myself, described elsewhere. I do not believe that he had told Helen that he did not wish to go over the proofs with me, as Helen stated in her book. In looking back, however, it was perhaps better that I had no responsibility for *The Bulwark* in its final stage. I knew that there had been changes, but I should have trusted the odd destiny that had brought the book so far, to complete the work. I had been particularly eager to see that at least in this important novel of Dreiser's, there should be no changes in his style. The proofs, as I saw them later, were practically untouched, yet I could quote some transposition of sentences and the omission of several extraordinary literary lines.[73]

Scarcely a week later, I came home from work and found my son looking very tense: "Helen phoned that Dreiser died," he muttered, he himself deeply moved. "She said you could come down."[74]

As I arrived at King's Road, an ambulance-type hearse was at the door. I went in the house and embraced Helen, just as the men were wheeling out the large figure, covered with a sheet. "Do you want to see him?" Helen asked. "I'd like to ride with him, if you don't mind," I answered. She said nothing, and I followed the men out with him. There was a low seat beside the stretcher, and it seemed perfectly natural to sit beside him, as I had often done with patients in the Red Cross ambulances.[75]

Dreiser had been dead only about two hours, and he seemed fully there. We were alone together, as if in the center of a vibration which was almost joy. All the sorrow, the bitterness that I might have felt, was gone.

In the days immediately after Dreiser's death, I tried to be helpful to Helen. But she had other friends around her, including Dreiser's niece, Vera, whom she had summoned from New York. Allan Hunter came and agreed to conduct a funeral service, although he was aware that certain political friends thought a religious element was not necessary. But with his tact and liberal feelings, he was able to work out a plan for the ceremony with John Howard Lawson and Charlie Chaplin taking part.[76]

Except for talking with Allan, I was needed to do little by Helen. I don't know why there was such a delay in making all the arrangements, and it seemed unnatural to keep Dreiser's body a whole week in the Forest Lawn parlors, before it was taken to the Chapel of the Recessional. Would this make it more difficult for his spirit to leave the body?[77]

I had been to see him several times in his casket. Dressed in his dark lecturer's suit, with black bow tie, he was powerful and handsome in the nobility of death. His white hair and thick, dark eyebrows made the same contrast. If only his eyes would open, his gaze would most certainly have had the same old vigor and depth.

I had said good-bye to the silent figure, and the next morning, I was on my little patio where we had sat so many times; everything was lovely as usual, the flowers, the view of the distant hills, the sunlight, having in it the gift of life. I sat there in a daze, half-seeing, half-remembering. There was an hour before we had to leave for the Chapel at Forest Lawn. Suddenly, I felt that Dreiser was there beside me. I can't explain how. Just the fullness of his presence, completely real. I did not want to move, flooded with an inner gladness. Time seemed suspended. But then I realized it was getting late.

"Come, Teddy, we have to go to the funeral," I said, out loud, and he got up with me. Then he was gone, and I got into my car with my son, to follow him to the chapel.

After this interlude on the patio, and because I had grown to love my little house, as did my son, we decided to stay there for the rest of the winter, until the end of the school year. As for me, there could be no better place to write about the previous year with Dreiser and our work together on *The Bulwark*. And so the last half of my first Dreiser book was written there, where I could freshly remember all the details.

Strangely enough, Helen did not want to see me, though I called her several times. One day, she drove up, when she knew no one was there, and left some books, and the plaster mould of the death mask made at my suggestion by the sculptor Edgardo Simone. As if she did not wish to keep the mask herself. Simone had made a head of Dreiser some time before, and I knew that sculptors, especially Italians, are trained to make such masks, which are often indescribably effective.[78]

On that visit to my empty house, Helen left me a note saying that she did not wish to see me at the moment, as she was still very upset by Dreiser's death, but that she would get in touch with me at a later time. This she never did, and I was truly sorry, as I felt I had always been fair and open with her.

A sad thing that after Dreiser's death, Helen did not seem able to reap the full rewards and honors of being his widow. After all the frustrations and difficulties of her life, she was determined to become a personality in her own right. She tried to get singing engagements, and lived carelessly in Hollywood, alienating most of her best companions. On a trip to New York, she saw her old friend Ralph Fabri, and he was distressed at her apparent recklessness. A young man from Hollywood had accompanied her, and she seemed nervous and confused. She had, however, done two valuable things to preserve Dreiser's work and image. Under her supervision, all of his files and eventually his possessions were sent to the University of Pennsylvania to establish a special collection, a disposal that Dreiser had initiated earlier. And she wrote, with some assistance, her own book, about her life with him.

Whatever technical help she may have had, Helen's book is her own record of her life, mostly forthright and honest in its portrayal of her emotions and spiritual struggles. It also gives a colorful if fragmentary account of Dreiser's life over a period of some thirty years, with many characteristic incidents and remarks which make him live before the reader's eye and ear. There is a simple store of direct, significant detail, and not the mass of facts, accumulated by certain biographers, that overwhelm the reader but give no clear picture, not even the ugly and cynical one that some critics exhibited. But Helen truly understood him, and loved him, only too well. And for this, her own life had a special significance.

In 1951, in Hollywood, Helen had a severe stroke. She was partially paralyzed and lost her power of speech. Her devoted sister, Myrtle, summoned from up north, arranged Helen's affairs as well as she could and took her in an ambulance back to her own ranch near Gresham, Oregon, where she lived with her husband. She had been married to this substantial, hearty rancher at about the same time that Helen had secretly married Teddy.[79] In Oregon with her sister, Helen lived quite content, as Myrtle wrote me, although she could not leave her wheelchair and never regained her speech. But Myrtle sent me photographs showing a happy family on the ranch, with Helen smiling graciously from her wheelchair, in a charming long gown.

Helen died in Oregon. I believe she left at least some of her money to an African-American orphanage, as Dreiser had requested. Myrtle accompanied her body to Hollywood, where it rests by Dreiser's on the wooded knoll of Forest Lawn. Her final place beside him can never be taken away.

The multiplicity of Dreiser's interests had its source in his search for truth. At first it would seem to be an eagerness to learn everything he could about human nature: what made people act the way they did? What were the forces that influenced them or controlled them? Few novelists have looked as deeply into the characters and experiences of women, in order to understand them, as Dreiser did. Not stopping with his full-length fictional studies of Carrie Meeber, Jennie Gerhardt, or Roberta Alden, he collected stories partly written by his heroines themselves, in his *A Gallery of Women*.[80] Although this was not a particularly successful volume, he still thought in terms of using confessional stories to explore further the psychology of the female of the species. As late as his last year, he said he would like to collect a series of tales to be entitled *Why Women Leave Their Husbands,* because of a friend who had just left a rich rancher with a beautiful home, after only a few months of marriage.

But it was not only the psychology of women that interested him. He also painted a gallery of varied masculine portraits. Take his exhaustive study of one man, Charles Yerkes, ruthless capitalist and philanderer, which ran through three books, *The Financier, The Titan,* and *The Stoic*. With his male characters, he entered more easily into the fields of speculation, politics, or religion, and finally, scientific information. Dreiser was always open to the ideas of others, although he might hotly contest those with whom he could not agree. He liked to test out his ideas in discussion. But he preferred to argue about politics or religion with men, or to exchange facts with minds of his own, inquiring bent. In fact, Dreiser said that he had found his most stimulating friendships among men, not women. Perhaps because his relationships with women were inevitably colored by sex attraction, or the lack of it, he felt greater freedom in the clean-cut companionship of men.

One of those men, John Cowper Powys, knew about Dreiser's great project of writing the philosophy of his life, and had read many of the notes that Dreiser had written, as well as his earlier essays in *Hey-Rub-a-Dub-Dub*.[81] They had many discussions as to the mysteries of existence, the psychic forces of which each was so constantly aware. So Powys always encouraged Dreiser to go on to complete this new work and eagerly consented to write an introduction for it. By the following June, Powys had started to do so. After Dreiser's sudden death, Jack and Phyllis wrote to Helen showing his deep concern lest some press or editor should get hold of the *Notes,* and contort them in some way. He knew how Dreiser's work had sometimes been injured by well-meaning editors. And so he urged Helen to do the editing without any help except the publisher's:

June 28, 1946

My most dear Helen,

How your Phyllis & John do love these exciting and beautiful letters from you. Phyllis and I were & *are* still I can tell you *very thrilled* over this grand resolution and determination and fixed project of yours to get these 17 essays and these casual notes for some philosophical book, printed and published as soon as possible! If I were you—(for Phyllis and I are deeply concerned with your most naturally paralysed and dazed and numbed and petrified state.) *Protem* We don't think you must let it last any longer—We think, O so strongly, that you must burst these bands and strike out boldly for his spirit and his influence and his glory without end, and his effect for GOOD untold on the world and on the individual souls throughout all time-

We think you would be wiser *not* to get any help at all from anybody *except the publishers* you *select* and their appointed official editors—*No Body* else!

And for God's sake my dear girl and P. joins O so gravely with me here—Do NOT put these precious things in a University!

The world doesn't want, posterity doesn't want some *other person's views on him* or *views on his philosophy!* Or this *other's* attempts to give these notes a *rounding off* to suit *his* or *their* alien ideas!

The world—or rather thousands and thousands of *Individuals* in the world—want to *have in their hands Dreiser himself* his own notes however fragmentary! and *then* each individual can form *his own notion* of what Dreiser (your Theodore) *meant.*

Phyllis and I (if we were you Helen dear) would get hold of the publisher and *nobody else* and make your arrangements with them, *alone*—And don't bring anyone else into it! Persuade him to publish all these finished essays in one volume and *with them* all these scattered fragments and these notes—such as you quote here in this letter—Yes, yes, certainly! Just these notes or these single words in a list as you put them here. Strength and Weakness, Myth of Responsibility, The Factor called Chance, Necessity for Contrast, Necessity for Limitation, Necessity for Secrecy, Courage and Fear, The Problem of Knowledge, Theory that Life is a Game, Problem of Death. Yes, let the publisher print *a couple of pages* of these, at the end of the finished essays, entitling them *"From Dreiser's Note-Books"*. I am absolutely certain that such a book—edited by you *alone,* Dreiser's Philosophy edited by Helen Dreiser would satisfy all of us individuals (100's of us! who are so stirred by his terrific elemental, multiversial, mysterious planetary genius—in a way we shall not be—and could *never* be if you brought in anyone else, even if the person were very clever and quite a thinker!

We Want Theodore and his Helen and *No Body Else!*

Yours as heretofore and as hereafter—

We feel that Quaker book of his was *first rate!*

O how tender he was to all his characters in it!

Ever your loyal and faithful and affectionate.[82]

As a matter of fact, Helen did not feel capable of editing the tremendous file of the *Notes on Life* herself. She entrusted the work to a young scholar who undertook to do just what Powys had feared. Not understanding Dreiser's essential way of thinking, which was not academic or logical, according to most organized philosophies, but rather, literary and spiritual, this scholar tried to press the whole work into an intellectual mold completely alien to its purpose, which was to ask questions, arouse speculation, and propose vast concepts without hidebound conclusions. This scholar's redrafted outlines can be found in the University of Pennsylvania files of *Notes on Life*. Unfortunately for him, but fortunately for Dreiser's work, he took sick and died at a premature age.[83]

A last word about *The Notes on Life* and their relevance to Dreiser's deepest beliefs. The *Notes* represent the culmination of his thinking about life and love. In the 1930s he began to read scientific books, to visit laboratories and observatories, and to hold long discussions with scientists. He had engaged the young college-girl secretary, Harriet Bissell, to help him specifically with this work. Dreiser never hesitated to credit her with a brilliant mind. Knowing what he had in prospect, she read through dozens of books for him, to locate scientific data which he could use for illustration. She also arranged interviews for him, with some outstanding scientists whose books were particularly interesting. These scientists responded to his eagerness to know, and found that he seemed to have an intuitive ability to grasp general principles, so that even though he did not understand all details, nor all terminology, he could rejoice in discoveries and see their human import. Not science fiction but science literature was his quarry, truth that could be translated into beauty or surprise, stirring the complacent mind.

Scientists who talked with Dreiser, and allowed him to question them, understood this individual attitude of his and found him good company. There was something about his personality that offered a rare kind of attention. They sensed he was as creative in his field as they were in theirs.

Dreiser was in the midstream of his life when he started the research and formulation for his new book. He was then eager to accept all scientific proof, all agnostic theories which in the first part of our century made it seem as though the enlightened mind must choose between science and religion as irreconcilable opposites. But Dreiser also believed in change, and he was living in an age of great changes. Certain scientists—Einstein and Arthur Compton, among others—began to find a relationship between science and a Creator, or at least some free, Creative Force.[84] Dreiser with them and many other thinkers of the time moved into an area of broader horizons. He was plodding in the same direction as the articulate and brilliant Frenchman, Teilhard de Chardin, with his mastery of science.[85] He was seeking the pattern of the life process—a *mechanism,* directed by something that was not mechanical, but inscrutable, powerful, and benevolent.

Nature, Force, Creator. Humbly, he regarded these phenomena from every side. Dreiser's philosophy as it developed out of his *Notes* followed no formal pattern but was a further projection of that constant curiosity and search for realities that had characterized his entire life.

The originality of his mind was always surprising. As an ordinary gathering of people around him might turn into an extraordinary dialogue or a fascinating monologue concerning some recent discovery, so from the springboard of a scientific fact or observation, a long, eloquent *note* might follow, opening up a wide cosmic view, or powerful literary expression of some new truth. His philosophy was part of his lifestyle, his awareness, his deep desire to understand the forces operating around him.

As his work had progressed, more and more scientific facts and possibilities for illustrations presented themselves. Harder and harder to make an end of it, but his general outline was determined. He had wished to weave each chapter into a strong essay containing many shorter notes. Sometimes he could not decide where to place a note and so had copies filed under several different headings. I cannot help feeling that if he had tried to fit all these notes into larger frames, many would have been left out. Some of the shorter notes, as they appear alone, are very like the remarks or ideas that he would bring out in his rich, inimitable conversations about life.

So, in considering Dreiser's *Notes,* one should remember that while many are essays or fragments of powerful writing, they are also expressions of his temperament and talent as he projects them in his novels and poetry. They are a virtually untapped but intrinsic part of his literary biography. They have been, so far, the least known of his writings. Dreiser's constant questioning, however, sets his *Notes* apart from those of Thoreau, the great naturalist of Walden, who influenced Dreiser deeply in the novelist's formative years. Certainly, the older writer encouraged Dreiser's already strong love and reverence for nature. But he quoted very little of Thoreau in his *Notes on Life*. He did, however, make excellent use of certain philosophical statements that appear elsewhere in a frame not specifically naturalistic. Thoreau's world was Walden and the forests and the rivers of New England. Dreiser did not keep the same concentration, but his mind traveled over the world of information, seeking natural phenomena wherever they appeared in his reading if they seemed appropriate to make some philosophic point of his own.

Under Emotions come the notes on love and sex. Looking back to these, you might almost say that the longer ones could have come from one of Dreiser's serious novels where he is analyzing the force and the fragility of love. Here is one where he returns to scientific concepts, yet manages to make a startling statement about the passion of the Creator Himself:

> Love is an invisible, imponderable attractive force. It is the antonym of hate, repulsion. In chemistry it is called atomic affinity and is the basis or activating force of every chemical action; therefore, the very foundation of existence. For if the Creative Force as we know it, is basically matter-energy, atoms, ions or electricity and therefore God—the Creative Force is electrons, ions, protons, atoms, etc. harmonized and working together.
>
> In chemistry, these phases of matter-energy are called or are described as having atomic affinity and are therefore the base or activating force of every chemical action and therefore the foundation of existence. Thus, because hydrogen loves oxygen, we have water and so on, up the scale through the most complicated chemical reactions and the power of reason, love; attraction is the activating principle.
>
> Gravitation is the attraction or love of matter in mass; magnetism and electricity are manifestations of the primary force. In biology, it is the attraction of the opposite sex, the common or garden variety of which, and very often by some, is considered to be contaminated by passion, yet God or the Creative Force is, as you see, love and/or passion."[86]

In the chapter on "Beauty and Ugliness," as under "The Emotions," Dreiser extols the power of beauty in a woman. Her physical force generates the response of a man, almost as a current of electricity will light a lamp. Looking back over the *Notes on Life,* I am amazed at their richness. I love them myself, and hope to encourage others to read them. Those who know them already, I can only salute, and say: I do not understand them all; perhaps you do not. Dreiser himself says repeatedly that man is not equipped to grasp nor interpret the whole scene and functioning of the universe. The mystery is always deepening. But he has gone far into it, with illuminating probes and reactions that make this reading a profound experience of fact, fantasy, and literary art. In any case, the difficulty of following some of his ideas is counteracted by their richness and variety, not to mention the originality of his concepts. His theory of contrasts and balances becomes a fascinating addition to anyone's philosophy.

Even the very subtle remarks about change and *interest,* as contrasted with a stultifying sameness or *ennui,* as he calls it, are very typical of Dreiser's own mind. Boredom was, to his wide, restless nature, an actual pain from which he could not always easily escape. In younger days, it led to some of his deep depressions. In his last California period, he was able to retreat, mentally, into the consoling meditations of his garden.

A strong feeling of gratitude for the bounty of God, expanding into love, is found in Dreiser's later writings. In "The Salve Called Religion," he wrote:

> When man realizes that he is a planned and created mechanism, the handiwork of his creator, and that in the *plan*—the totality of its structure and movement—is discernibly *no intended evil,* at least not to man himself, the extension and instrument of his creator; that there is in the mechanistic process a balance and proportion, which seemingly without imbalance or disorder involves and permits of love and hate, mercy and cruelty, sorrow and joy, good and evil, ugliness and beauty, truth and falsehood, justice and injustice, ends and beginnings, strength and weakness, courage and fear, ignorance and wisdom, frankness and secrecy, plus interest and ennui, one can, without religious or dogmatic delusions, experience awe, reverence, gratitude, and, more, love for so wondrous a process or spirit, whichever one chooses to emphasize.[87]

In his very accurate and balanced way, Dreiser was trying to put down all the contrasts and possibilities that make this life so colorful and dramatic, if also dangerous. He had always met his destiny head on, suffered it and also exulted in it. And he had always sought to understand, to explain, to grow closer to the truth. He felt that he had finally come very near it. But he still did not have the presumption to think that he had found all the answers, nor unveiled all the wonders. So he had been satisfied to call his work simply *Notes on Life*. But that life was ever more precious to him, and in his last years something grew in his spirit, which was more than knowledge. It was an experience of the Creator of all this Bounty which he expressed in a type of note slipped into his files, and hardly belonging to his organized chapters.

Working with Dreiser's material, I have felt, more and more, the persuasion of his general ideas, the sweep and beauty of his imagination, and the courage of his lifelong confrontation with the Unknown. I have looked back on our friendship with a profound sense of gratitude and wonder at the destiny that seemed to operate in our lives, bringing us together when we could be useful to each other, although, particularly in the beginning, we treated our encounters in the most haphazard manner.

Sometimes I regret that I did not ask him more questions about his work and thoughts. For often, when I dropped in to see him in his garden, in the late afternoon, he would have a pencil in his hand, and paper nearby. He would look up, his eyes full of life, scowling, smiling, changing as they always did. "Sit down, I want to tell you something," he would say, taking my hand with affection, but it was usually about some bird, or news of the day. He seldom talked about his *Notes on Life*. He did not seem to worry about them. He knew his files would be preserved and he believed in his own theory of a Creative Force that could bring his work to completion, if such were its wish. What he had written, he had written, and he still hoped to get back to it. But this was not the time. He was filled with such a sense of the present, one might almost say of the presence of the present, a vertical escape from time, that merely being with him was freedom from all worries and frustrations—a joy complete in itself. Though many of his meditations in the garden during those last days must have been lost, absorbed in the sunlight, or fallen into the silence of the grass, the novels and other writings he has left us form a priceless literary legacy.

Editor's Notes

1. *The Bulwark* (Garden City, N.Y.: Doubleday, 1946), 244. This posthumously published novel chronicles Quaker protagonist Solon Barnes's mostly unavailing attempts to shield his children from the temptations of American materialism.
2. Maxwell was a copy editor for the *Chicago Globe* when Dreiser met him in 1892. In the same year he met McCullagh, the editor and famed editorial writer for the *St. Louis Globe-Democrat*. Dreiser's brother Paul (Dresser) left the family home in Terre Haute to become the musical toast of Broadway, the famed composer of "My Gal Sal," "On the Banks of the Wabash," "My Mother Told Me So," and "The Blue and the Gray."
3. *A Book About Myself* (New York: Boni and Liveright, 1922), 27. An uncut version of this autobiography was published under the title *Newspaper Days* by the University of Pennsylvania Press in 1991.
4. Sarah White at age twenty-four was more than two years the future novelist's senior when they met aboard a Chicago-bound train in 1893. "Jug," as she was nicknamed, came from Montgomery City, Missouri, to teach in the St. Louis suburb of Florissant. Both travelers were on their way to the Chicago World's Fair, she to partake of its educational benefits, he to cover it for the *St. Louis Republic*. In a short time Dreiser was enmeshed, going so far as to construct a miniature shrine in his room to venerate his new love.
5. *A Book About Myself,* 423–28.
6. Kirah Markham was a twenty-year-old amateur painter and actress of great beauty. Dreiser met her in 1913 when she was with the Little Theater in Chicago. Helen Patges married an actor named Frank Richardson when she was sixteen. She was twenty-five, separated, and

an aspiring actress when she met Dreiser in 1919. She became the novelist's long-standing mistress and his second wife in 1944.

7. Laetitia MacDonald Irwin, 1890–1965, was the author of novels including *The Young and the Fair* (1933), *Silver Platter* (1934), and *Golden Hammock* (1951), as well as a dozen short stories that appeared in a variety of magazines including *Smart Set*. Dwight MacDonald (1906–82) was at the time an editor and critic. He later wrote for the *Partisan Review* and founded the pacifist journal *Politics* (1944–49). He also wrote for the *New Yorker* and for *Esquire* as a film critic. Among his books are *Henry Wallace: The Man and the Myth* (1948) and *Memoirs of a Revolutionist* (1957). He was a vocal opponent of World War II and the Vietnam War. Maria Jolas was the wife of Eugene Jolas (1894–1952), a journalist and editor born in Loraine and remembered most for his fostering of avant-garde literature. *Transition* magazine, which the Jolases initiated in Paris during 1927, published experimental literature. It evolved into a reliable outlet for symbolists and surrealists. Between 1927 and 1930, excerpts from James Joyce's *Finnegan's Wake* appeared in *Transition*. The magazine ceased publication in 1938. Wallace Irwin (1875–1959) gained prominence with his book of verse *Love Sonnets of a Hoodlum* in 1902. He also wrote detective stories and a novel about the difficulties of integration encountered by the Japanese in California titled *Seed of the Sun* (1921).
8. During Tjader's final year at Barnard College, where she was studying the fine arts, she met her future husband, Overton (Tony) Harris. He had been an officer on a destroyer in World War I. After a period of company-keeping, Harris followed Tjader on one of her numerous trips to her birthplace, Stockholm, and proposed. They were married in 1922 despite Tjader's misgivings. Harris took up his practice as a high-powered attorney in the frenetic days before the stock-market crash of 1929. Tjader divorced Harris in Switzerland in 1933.
9. Dreiser and Helen lived in the Rodin Studios at 200 West Fifty-seventh Street from December 1926 until September 1931. Moving to the thirteenth floor duplex was mostly Helen's idea. Dreiser regarded the rent, originally quoted at $4,000 per year and reduced at the novelist's insistence to $3,500, as scandalously wasteful. After a time, however, he came to appreciate the place with its large foyer, cathedral ceiling, and stained-glass windows fronting Fifty-seventh Street. The studio might have become Dreiser's permanent residence had it not been rendered beyond his means by the loss of much of the profit from *An American*

Tragedy in the stock-market crash of 1929.

10. Tjader's father had died in December of 1916. An unpublished Tjader autobiography identifies the French lover only as Pierre, an officer of the French line. The two met on Tjader's return trip from Stockholm after her tentative engagement to Tony Harris. They rendezvoused clandestinely once in 1929, but the affair broke off in 1930 when the Frenchman took offense at Tjader's attempt to see him in Nantes where he lived with his family.
11. Dreiser met Powys while the former was researching the Cowperwood trilogy in Chicago in early 1913. Powys's family was descended from ancient Welsh princes. His father, Charles Francis Powys, was a clergyman, three of whose sons, John Cowper, Theodore Francis, and Llewelyn were literary figures. Another son, Albert Reginald, was an honored architect. John Cowper's most successful novels were *Wood and Stone* (1915) and *Wolf Solent* (1929). His poetry included, in addition to *Samphire, Wolfsbane,* and *Mandragora,* an epic called *Lucifer,* written in 1905 but unpublished until 1955. He also wrote works of criticism such as *Visions and Revisions* and *The Meaning of Culture.* John Cowper Powys died in 1963 at age ninety-one.
12. *Notes on Life* was a compilation of observations about existence that Dreiser culled form his readings in literature, science, and the popular media. Tjader's edited version (with John McAleer) was published by the University of Alabama Press in 1974, with an introduction by John Cowper Powys. The unpublished *Notes* that Tjader quotes in this book are preserved in the University of Pennsylvania's Dreiser Collection. The quote from Lawrence was one of many comparisons the English novelist made between what he called "mind consciousness" and "blood consciousness." He believed that Western civilization had cultivated the former, the rational and scientific side of man, while allowing the latter, the primitive, sensual, and intuitive side, to atrophy.
13. *The Natural Philosophy of Love,* trans. Ezra Pound, (London: The Casanova Society, 1926), 124–25.
14. "The Lost Phoebe" was finished in 1912 but rejected nineteen times by magazines until accepted by *Century* in 1915. The story is often anthologized to this day, though its theme of undying love and devotion to one partner makes it antithetical to almost everything else Dreiser wrote.
15. Hilary Harris, Tjader's only child, later became an honored documentary-film maker. His major works include *Highway,* the winner of the

1958 Brussels Fair bronze medal and the 1959 Locarno Film Festival Diploma of Honor; *Seawards the Great Ships,* which garnered sixteen international awards including the 1962 Academy Award for best short subject; *Organism,* recipient of the Blue Ribbon of the American Film Festival in 1976; and numerous other productions.

16. Tjader's novel *Borealis* was brought out by the New York publishing house of Logos in 1931. After she showed Dreiser the manuscript, he supplied a blurb for its publication praising its "honest analysis of character" and pronouncing it the product of a "moody, changeful, sensitive mind." Dreiser's praise is, in fact, justified. The novel, despite its subsequent neglect, holds up quite well. And a synopsis of its situations and actions reveals something of the influence of Dreiser on Tjader, as well as her own philosophy of sex.

Borealis follows the development of an "unreasonably impressionable" Swedish child into an introspective and free-spirited woman of thirty. The opening section, subtitled "Adolescence," is set in the countryside near Stockholm. Signe, the young heroine, fears yet wonders at Grolle, an enormous stallion that inhabits a neighboring farm. The great horse becomes a symbol for Signe's emerging fascination with eroticism, a characteristic further focused when she chances upon a scene of farm folk coupling in the midnight sun.

The main plot of the book begins with Signe the mother of an eight-year-old son and twenty-nine on the afternoon of her tenth wedding anniversary. She has been living a reasonably happy, fast society life full of charming flirtations. Her husband, Anders, numbers several extramarital affairs among his own experiences. Signe sees both her own and her husband's dalliances as a natural concomitant of their longing for fulfillment. "It was morally wrong to waste things . . . that was one of the strongest arguments Signe used on herself when she was contemplating some new step in matters of emotion" (45). At this point in the story her affair with a man named Erich is winding down as her interest in Arvid Garde quickens. The charismatic Garde, perhaps a character inspired by Dreiser, has been urging her to change her ways, offering her a shared life of passion for its own sake. She considers divorcing her husband whose love had changed "into a sort of brotherly affection" (100). But a friend's admonition that no man can feel the same about a woman he has lived with for a long time leads her to apply the maxim to Garde as well as to her husband. Brooding over the situation reinforces her carpe diem approach to living, as do recurring reminders of death. Her own near drowning during a trip with Garde further strengthens her resolve to live adventurously but also intensifies her conviction that existence equals tragedy for both sexes: "Life beats everyone in the end, but most men go down ignominiously, because they fight many things at once. With a woman it is a little different. A woman is born to be destroyed . . . some one thing will destroy her, a man, children, or money, or an idea outside of herself . . . whatever she chooses to love. Men fight for love, or money, or an idea of their own, but they are wounded or killed . . . they are not destroyed like a woman is, from the root. . . . And if a woman cannot choose a force to which to give herself over, then old age will destroy her, and that is worst of all, because it means she has been afraid of everything else" (199–200).

Signe decides to break up with Arvid because, though she has loved him "body and soul, " she knows that the inevitable drifting into an "impersonal current" must follow such strong passion. During the lovers' breakup scene, the two become drunk and Garde accused Signe of prostitution because she cannot be satisfied with one man. His rage turns violent and he physically abuses her. When he sobers up he makes brutal love to her but she knows it is a culmination, not a new beginning. ". . . their lovemaking was a sacrificial rite in a tragic religion which they believed without knowing why. . . . Their very sensuality became the humbling of themselves before some unforgiving God of Finality." Signe returns the next day to her home and family, certain that "the poignancy of the last night had been the pinnacle of her life," (224) and determined to spend the rest of her days on the lower and lonely rocks of renunciation.

At best one can only speculate as to the specifics behind Dreiser's cryptic critique of *Borealis* in his letter to Tjader. The seeming caveat that the book is concentric and personal may derive from his preference for the large canvas depicting clashes of forces, characters, and points of view over her filtering of events through the sensibility of a central intelligence. The same preference may account for Dreiser's feeling that the dramatic dimensions of Tjader's novel were insufficient, though from another perspective *Borealis* might be vulnerable to attack on the ground that it becomes overly dramatic. But the criticism of the novel's ending proves the most provocative of Dreiser's reactions. It could indicate that he discerned a logical flaw in the heroine's ultimate rejection of extramarital relationships. Tjader makes that rejection flow out of Signe's realization that passion is short-lived, but the novel effectively argues that transient relationships are preferable to emotional contraction. Or Dreiser's finding the ending less than compelling may have been a simple gut reaction to Signe's seemingly definitive embrace of renunciation, a denouement that might have pleased Henry James, but never Dreiser.

The final paragraph of Dreiser's letter may reveal his suspicion that Tjader had appropriated some of his free-thinking in creating the promiscuous heroine of her novel. Whether the suspicion was well founded or not, evidence can be detected in *Borealis* for subtler similarities in the emotional makeup of both Dreiser and Tjader. Beyond the interest in sexual varietism, for example, Signe's creator assigns her a pervasive brooding over life's inherent tragedy, a trait that the correspondence in the present volume shows Tjader shared with Dreiser. Moreover, Signe also professes a deep but undifferentiated compassion for the downtrodden but accompanies her feeling with no commensurate actions to help them. Both Dreiser and Tjader felt and hesitated similarly until the middle and late 1930s when events spurred Dreiser to act on behalf of various humanitarian causes and Tjader to found *Direction* magazine as a voice for social justice. In these and other ways, Dreiser and Tjader shared a view of life that made her, of all his women, the closest to a soul mate.

17. With some of the profits from the brisk sales of *An American Tragedy,* Dreiser had bought in 1927 a thirty-seven-acre tract of land that overlooked Croton Lake near Mount Kisco, New York. The next year he began directing the construction of a large house on the property, which had only a couple of primitive cabins on it when he bought it. Numerous changes in design were made as the house took shape. So many, in fact, that the place became an object of puzzled curiosity to the inhabitants of the area. W. A. Swanberg in his 1965 biography *Dreiser* (New York: Charles Scribner's Sons) attributes the bewildering appearance of the house to the imaginations of at least four other artists besides Fabri, including Wharton Esherick, Jerome Blum, Henry Varnum Poor, and Habert Davis. Actually, Fabri was brought into the design process late in the going, prompting him to remark that Dreiser's was the first house he had ever known to have been "built from the roof down" (Swanberg, 357).

    As to how the name "Iroke" came to be chosen for the retreat, there is no definitive answer. Dreiser apparently heard from someone, perhaps from his sister Sylvia's husband, a Japanese-American named Kishina, that the word conjured up the idea "beauty" in Japanese. The standard transliterated spelling of the word is actually "iroke," though the sound of the final syllable "e" may sometimes be pronounced "i" in some Japanese dialects, particularly those spoken in areas north of Tokyo. Dreiser's biographers characteristically simply gloss the meaning of "Iroke" as beauty and ignore the intriguing actual first connotation of the word in Japanese. "Iroke" functions almost invariably as a description of woman's sexual attractiveness, sexuality, seductiveness. Etymologically, the morpheme "iro" means "color"; "ke," sometimes pronounced "ke" (this is not a dialectical variation), means "spirit," "mind," "heart." Thus, literally "iroke" can be translated to "the spirit of color." The word *color* in Japanese connotes sex. There may have been some misunderstanding in Dreiser's naming the house, since an inanimate object cannot possess "iroke." Or Dreiser may have intentionally broadened the meaning for his own purposes, which certainly would have been understandable given his proclivities.

I am indebted to one of my former Japanese students, Shoko Emori, for putting me on to the real meaning of the term, to Professor Kiyohiko Myrayama of Hitosubashi University in Tokyo and Professor Yoshinobu Hakutani of Kent State University for the additional linguistic information, and to the novelist's niece, Dr. Vera Dreiser, for the conjecture about the role of Sylvia's husband in Dreiser's choice of the name.

Dreiser lived off and on at Iroki until it was sold in 1944 while he was a permanent resident in Hollywood. For the most complete account of Iroki and Dreiser's use of it, see W. A. Swanberg's *Dreiser*, 381–501 passim.

Dreiser's friend Ralph Fabri was born in Budapest in 1894. He studied at the Royal Academy of Fine Arts there before coming to the United States in 1921. He became a naturalized U.S. citizen and taught at City College of New York while producing paintings and etchings that earned him national and international exhibitions and numerous prizes. He died in 1975.

18. Nathan and Boyd conceived the idea of a literary newspaper to be called the *American Spectator* in 1932. Nathan had edited the *American Mercury* with H. L. Mencken during the twenties. Nathan was best known then as a drama critic and is remembered today mostly for his later book *The Entertainment of a Nation* (1942). He died in 1958. Boyd was an Irish critic and essayist who had served as a member of

the editorial staff of the *New York Evening Post* in the twenties and earlier as British Counsel in Spain. His books include *Ireland's Literary Renaissance* (1916, 1922) and *Studies in Ten Literatures* (1925). He died in 1946. Cabell was a novelist who first gained notoriety with the temporary suppression of Jurgen, a fantasy that, like Dreiser's *The 'Genius'* (1915), pioneered a more open approach to sex in literature. Cabell died in 1958. The original organization of the *American Spectator* called for Boyd to function as managing editor with Nathan as working editor and Cabell, Dreiser, Sinclair Lewis, and O'Neill on the editorial board. The first issue appeared in November of 1932. Differences with the editorial board led Dreiser to resign his post in January of 1934.

19. The magazine to which Tjader alludes here and about which she elaborates later in this book was *Direction*. A self-avowed "antifascist" publication, the magazine ran from December 1937 through the summer issue of 1944. Originally mounted as a monthly based in Tjader's Darien, Connecticut, home, *Direction* was forced during several phases of its existence to revert to quarterly appearances. Its shifting roster of editors included over its six-plus-year run John Hyde Preston, Thomas Cochran, Dreiser secretary Harriet Bissell, H. L. River, William Gropper, Martin Kanin, and Tjader.

Several of Tjader's editor colleagues were avowed communists or sympathizers and members of the League of American Writers, the cultural front organization of the Communist Party of America. Gropper, the best known of the group, for example, was a popular cartoonist and artist who got his start with the *Yiddish Communist Daily* in New York City and later worked for *Masses* and its successors *Liberator* and *New Masses*. Though Gropper consistently denied he was a Communist, he did take the 5th Amendment before the McCarthy hearings in 1953. *Direction*'s list of contributors constitutes a glittering galaxy. Many of America's and some of the world's most important left-wing writers and artists appeared in it during the decade before the end of World War II. They include in addition to Dreiser, who provided the Foreword to the first issue: John Dos Passos; noted drama critic John W. Gassner who for several years contributed a regular column on the American stage; French (born in Switzerland) architect Le Corbusier (pseudonym of Charles Edouard Jeanneret); Erskine Caldwell; critic Kenneth Rexroth; Sherwood Anderson; Kenneth Burke; Russian commentator Vladimir Pozner; photographer Margaret Bourke White; Ernest

Hemingway; Van Wyk Brooks; Granville Hicks; S. J. Perelman; social historian George Selden; poet and critic Jean Starr Untermeyer; Ralph Ellison; theologian Paul Tillich; Berthold Brecht; broadcaster Raymond Gram Swing; Langston Hughes; Charlie Chaplin; Richard Wright; Glenway Westcott; and Carl Sandburg. Special issues were devoted to works by writers involved in various federally sponsored writing programs. Dreiser's contributions to *Direction* as well as the one acknowledged essay Tjader wrote for the magazine are reproduced in Appendix B.

20. Horace Brisbin Liveright with Albert Boni founded the publishing firm of Boni and Liveright in 1918. Liveright served as president of the company between 1918 and 1930. Dreiser had contractual relations with Liveright during this period starting with the reissue of *Sister Carrie*. In 1922 Boni and Liveright purchased the rights to all of his books, thus unknowingly positioning themselves to profit from the lucrative publication of *An American Tragedy* in 1925. A year earlier, Liveright had begun theatrical producing and by 1930 was employed by Paramount after having steered *An American Tragedy* to the studio for filming. The quarrel that ensued between the novelist and the publisher over Joseph von Sternberg's 1931 movie version of *An American Tragedy* (filmed after Sergei Eisenstein's adaptation of the novel was aborted) marked the culmination of their often stormy relationship. For a fuller discussion of the controversy surrounding the Eisenstein and von Sternberg adaptations, see my essay "Squandered Possibilities: The Film Versions of Dreiser's Novels" in *Theodore Dreiser: Beyond Naturalism,* ed. Miriam Gogol (New York: New York University Press, 1995). Tjader seems to have taken Dreiser's side of the quarrel between the novelist and Liveright, though there were, of course, two sides to the story.
21. This letter is not among those of Dreiser housed at the University of Pennsylvania, nor is it with those Tjader sold to the University of Texas. I have quoted it exactly as she has recorded it in her manuscript. The reference to Beppie alludes to a personal friend of Tjader's, Josef Rafenbaner.
22. Harriet Bissell was a Smith College alumnae who served as Dreiser's secretary from 1935 to 1938. Her major task during that time was researching and editing *The Living Thoughts of Thoreau,* the novelist's contribution to Longman's Green's Living Thoughts Series, and researching *Notes on Life*. She also served for a short time as an editor of

Tjader's magazine *Direction,* as indicated in my endnote 19.

23. Dreiser toured Harlan County during the first week in November of 1931 at a time when the Kentucky hill country was rent by violent clashes between miners and mine owners. He chaired a hearing arranged by the committee investigating conditions. A good deal of Dreiser's credibility with the public on the score of human rights violations uncovered in the hearing was shattered when local individuals, seeking to discredit him, caught him in a sexual indiscretion with a female traveling companion. His indictment for adultery by a Kentucky grand jury stole the headlines he had hoped to see devoted to the strikers and their exploiters.
24. Among the groups for which *Direction* provided a forum were the American League Against War and Fascism and the American Committee for Spanish Democracy. The WPA (Works Progress Administration) fostered and supported writing, drama, architecture, sculpture, and painting during Franklin D. Roosevelt's New Deal.
25. Calvin Bridges was a distinguished American geneticist at the California Institute of Technology. He and Dreiser met during the novelist's 1928 summer at Woods Hole laboratory in Massachusetts where Bridges was doing research.
26. The incident at Cold Spring Harbor that Tjader recounts here was one of two epiphanies that Dreiser thought crucial to the spiritual affirmation of his last years. The other was an encounter with a puff adder. While walking at Iroki one spring day in 1938, the novelist came upon the snake and killed it, thinking it was dangerous. When he saw another puff adder a few days later, he spoke with it and believed it understood his friendly intent. The two incidents tend to embarrass Dreiser apologists intent on valorizing him as a steadfast materialist.

    Cold Spring Harbor Biological Laboratory celebrated its centennial in 1990. James Dewey Watson, the laboratory's director for many years, did much of his ground-breaking work on DNA there.
27. Tjader's Connecticut estate, her residence at the time.
28. Madame Alma Clayburgh was an operatic soprano who had become by 1937 a noted sponsor of cultural and philanthropic causes. She was a successful concert singer under her maiden name (Lackenbruch) until 1908 when she married cotton broker Albert Clayburgh. At that point she retired from the stage and began aiding aspiring artists through musicales at her New York town house. After separating from her husband in 1916 she renewed her concert career under her professional

name, Alma Clayburgh. She retired definitively in 1931 and spent the rest of her life dedicated to causes, especially in the arts and including the Metropolitan Opera and the New York Symphony. She died in 1958 at the age of seventy-six.

Cosgrove had been editor of *Everybody's* magazine while Dreiser held the same position at the *Delineator* in 1909. Both magazines were Butterick publications targeted primarily to a female audience. Marian Powys Grey, John Cowper Powys's sister, was a world authority on old lace. John Golden was a theatrical producer who negotiated unsuccessfully to mount a production of Dreiser's play *The Girl in the Coffin* and a stage version of *The 'Genius.'* Arthur Carter Hume was Dreiser's New York lawyer at the time.

29. "Equity between Nations" was published in the September-October 1938 issue of *Direction*. See Appendix B. The version that appears in the magazine does not end with the passage to which Tjader alludes.
30. *Tragic America,* a polemic against what Dreiser regarded as rampant abuses by various institutions in this country, was published by Liveright in 1931. *America Is Worth Saving* argued that the United States should stay out of World War II. It was published by Modern Age Books in January of 1941.
31. The Spanish Militia, made up of volunteer fighters from all over the world and known thereafter as the International Brigades, took form in Spain beginning in 1936, despite many of the volunteers' home governments' policies of nonintervention in the "Civil War." The volunteers' object was to back the popularly elected government of the Spanish Republic against the aggression of Generals Franco, Mola, and Sanjuro in league with the Monarchists, Catholic CEDA, the Fascist Falange and external forces including 100,000 troops of the Italian Regular Army, the air force of Nazi Germany's "Condor Legion," and two divisions of the Regular Army of Portugal. The democratically inspired peoples of Spain held out against the inevitable with the help of the International Brigades for over two-and-a-half years. The Abraham Lincoln Battalion (known generally in the United States as the Lincoln Brigade) was the American arm of the International Brigades. Some 330 volunteers participated in the Lincoln Brigade during the course of the war. The most famous name connected with the brigade was that of Ernest Hemingway, who fought not with conventional weapons but rather with compelling dispatches from the front. The French novelist André Malraux was not a member of the Lincoln Brigade, as Tjader implies,

but the founder of the first International Air Squadron in Spain.

Dreiser's interview with Churchill was for a syndicated article. During their meeting, the novelist and the statesman mostly sparred over the merits of Russian Communism.

32. Dreiser met Henry in 1894. Henry was at the time the city editor for the *Toledo Blade*. He later helped Dreiser revise the rocking-chair scene that concludes *Sister Carrie*. Sterling was the author of "Spring in Carmel," "Autumn in Carmel," and "Beyond the Breakers." Dreiser and Sterling met through their mutual friend, H. L. Mencken. Sterling committed suicide by poison on November 17, 1926. Masters was the poet of *The Spoon River Anthology* (1915). His friendship with Dreiser spanned four decades.
33. Dreiser met Charles Fort (1874–1932) while the former was editing *Smith's* magazine, a Street and Smith venture, in 1905. Dreiser's acceptance of Fort's contributions marked the beginning of his persistent enthusiasm for the bizarre Albany writer whose later books catalogued strange occurrences beyond the powers of science to explain. Fort's books include *The Book of the Damned* (1919), *New Lands* (1923), and *Wild Talents* (1932). Dreiser was particularly taken with one of Fort's unpublished manuscripts called X, which posited that matter was created by mysterious cosmic rays. In 1931, Dreiser and other enthusiasts, including Indiana novelist Booth Tarkington and journalist-critic and Algonquin Hotel Round Table group leader Alexander Woolcott, formed the Fortean Society. In a move typical of Dreiser proselytizing for Fort, he sent *The Book of the Damned* to H. G. Wells only to have the English novelist pronounce its author "one of the most damnable bores who ever cut scraps from out-of-the-way newspapers and thought they were facts." Undaunted, Dreiser countered that he regarded the few printed copies of *The Book of the Damned* as "actual mental treasures to discriminating readers in many walks." (See Wells to Dreiser, April 9, 1931, and Dreiser to Wells, May 23, 1931, in Robert H. Elias, ed., *Letters of Theodore Dreiser* (Philadelphia: University of Pennsylvania Press, 1959), II, 531–33). Fort's inspiration doubtlessly led Dreiser to include his own researches into inexplicable phenomena among his *Notes on Life*.

Paul Robeson (1898–1976) had a brilliant career that began with the singing of African-American spirituals and progressed to distinguished acting on the New York stage as well as concert tours of Europe and motion-picture roles. His most famous vehicles included *The Emperor Jones, All God's Children, Porgy and Bess,* and *Othello.* Dreiser's sometimes interrupted friendship with H. L. Mencken (1880–1956) began when the former published the latter in the *Delineator,* one of the Butterick women's magazines, which Dreiser was editing in 1907.

34. Dreiser's *The 'Genius,'* with its thinly veiled autobiographical hero, artist Eugene Witla, had come under attack by the New York Society for the Suppression of Vice and other watchdog groups. The society's head, John Sumner, had discovered seventeen profane and seventy-five lewd passages in the book. In a rebuttal that was to prove a landmark in the fight against literary censorship, Mencken countered in the August 1917 issue of *Seven Arts,* pointing out that Sumner had overlooked several lewd and obscene snippets.
35. Powys, John Cowper, *Autobiography* (Norfolk, Connecticut: New Directions, 1960), 552–53, 554. In the same vein, Powys says elsewhere in *Autobiography:* "I am not a homo sexualist—I would shamelessly confess it to you, reader, if I were!—I am the extreme opposite of a narcissist or exhibitionist, but when I am attracted to something rugged, massive, primordial in men, men like my father, or my youngest brother Will, or Theodore Dreiser, I feel as if my emotion were exactly that of a young girl, tremulous with hero-worship." (426) And again: ". . . Dreiser, ever since I met him, which must have been in 1914 I think, struck me as a Being, as an Entity, who was profoundly conscious of his body, *and of what he put against his skin,* as he was conscious of the Corpus Terraqueous, and wherewithal *it* was fain to cover its cosmogonic bones. Dreiser struck me, in fact, as what you might call Matter—conscious or chemistry—conscious, to a degree that was almost non-human." (551, Powys's italics)
36. Tjader refers here to Powys's longtime, live-in friend, Phyllis Playter, by all accounts a charming and talented woman in her own right. Powys dedicated several of his books to Playter.
37. Powys to Dreiser, September 15, 1934. This is an excerpt from a longer letter in the University of Pennsylvania's Dreiser collection.
38. Arthur Neville Chamberlain was British prime minister from May 28, 1937, to May 10, 1940. His appeasement policy toward Germany is widely believed to have hastened and worsened World War II. Dreiser's reference to him in this letter predates by six weeks Chamberlain's

infamous meeting with French premier Edouard Daladier, Hitler, and Mussolini at Munich. On September 29 and 30, 1938, the four agreed there on the partition of Czechoslovakia.

39. Jones was a distinguished Quaker mystic regarded by Robert E. Spiller, Willard Thorp, et al., in their *Literary History of the United States,* Third Edition: Revised (New York: Macmillan, 1963) as "the most considerable thinker that American Quakerism has produced" (1,288). His major works were *Studies in Mystical Religion* and *Some Exponents of Mystical Religion* (both 1930). He was for most of his career professor of philosophy at Haverford College. The book to which Tjader refers here may have been either *Finding the Trail of Life* (1926) or *A Small Town Boy* (1941). Dreiser appropriated several incidents from these autobiographical accounts of Jones's youth to flesh out the story of Solon Barnes's boyhood in *The Bulwark.*
40. Mary Frances Dreiser (Mame), the eldest daughter of John Paul Dreiser and his wife Sarah, died in 1944 at the age of eighty-nine. Her seduction at age sixteen by a well-known Terre Haute lawyer inspired in part the title character in Dreiser's Jennie Gerhardt.
41. Benes was elected president of Czechoslovakia in 1935 and resigned the month following the incident Tjader describes, because of the German occupation of the Sudetenland. Benes left a promising career as a young professor to work in the Czech nationalist movement with philosopher Thomas Garrigué Masaryk between 1915 and 1919. He occupied a variety of government posts before his election to the presidency. After his resignation, he held a professorship at the University of Chicago and became president of the exile Czechoslovak government in England. When the war ended he returned to Czechoslovakia and was reelected president and served until his death in 1948.
42. Tjader's estate Vikingsborg on Tokeneke Trail in Darien, Connecticut.
43. Olin Downes was an eminent American music critic who wrote for the *Boston Post* (1906–24) and the *New York Times* from 1924 until the fifties. Art Young was a noted cartoonist and writer whose work was collected in *The Best of Art Young* (1936) and his biography, published under the title *Art Young: His Life and Times* (1939). Gilbert Wilson was an American painter whose portrait of Dreiser was unveiled at the Dreiser Centennial observances in Terre Haute in 1971. Critic and biographer Dorothy Dudley published *Forgotten Frontiers: Dreiser and the Land of the Free* in 1932.
44. The main house at Vikingsborg on Long Island Sound.

45. The address was 1015 North King's Road. Dreiser moved into the house with Helen on December 1, 1940, and lived there until his death on August 28, 1945.
46. Dreiser's only notable financial success from the project was the sale of the musical version of his sketch "My Brother Paul" to Twentieth-Century Fox. The price was in the range of $35,000 to $50,000, and Fox produced the movie under the title *My Gal Sal* for release in June of 1942. The brother in question was Paul Dresser, the noted songwriter who had changed his name from Dreiser to Dresser to disguise the German background he thought could hinder his career. He was born April 21, 1857, and died on January 30, 1906.
47. Dreiser's prose poem in praise of New York was published by Boni and Liveright in 1923.
48. Putnam became Dreiser's eighth American publisher in 1941. The "editor" to whom Tjader refers was actually Putnam vice president Earle Balch. Balch eventually became convinced that Dreiser would never deliver a satisfactory revision of *The Bulwark* and the novel eventually bore the Doubleday imprint when it was published posthumously in 1946.
49. Elizabeth Kearney. Her brother, Pat Kearney, had recently dramatized *An American Tragedy* on Broadway.
50. Helen Dreiser's book about her life with the novelist was issued by World Publishing Company (Cleveland and New York) in 1951.
51. See *Notes on Life,* 219–21.
52. Dreiser left New York for the West in November of 1938, stopping briefly at Helen's sister's house in Gresham, Oregon, outside Portland, and taking up residence in Glendale and then on North Hayworth Avenue in Hollywood before buying the King's Road house.
53. Tjader's letters to Dreiser are not among those housed at the University of Pennsylvania or at the University of Texas. I have quoted them directly from her manuscript version of this book.
54. Dreiser had been selected for the Award of Merit Medal and a $1,000 cash prize from the Academy for "extraordinary achievement in art" and "for breaking trail as a pioneer in the presentation in fiction of real human beings in a real America." (See presentation letter in Swanberg, 494). Unbeknownst to Dreiser, one of the instigators of his selection for the award was his old rival, Sinclair Lewis. The two had been involved in one of the more celebrated confrontations in American literary history. After a March 19, 1931, dinner honoring Russian novelist

Boris Pilnyak, Lewis rose to publicly accuse the glowering Dreiser of plagiarizing 3,000 words from his wife's (Dorothy Thompson's) book on Russia. Dreiser, already irked because Lewis rather than he had won the 1930 Nobel Prize for literature, responded by slapping Lewis repeatedly.

55. Actually, Dreiser and Helen were married June 13, 1944, at Stevenson, Washington, across the Columbia River and fifty miles east of Portland.
56. Elias's biography, begun while he was a graduate student at Columbia University in 1937, was published in 1948 by Alfred A. Knopf under the title *Theodore Dreiser: Apostle of Nature*. It remained the standard biography until the appearance of Swanberg's *Dreiser* in 1969. The definitive biography to date is the two-volume work of Richard Lingeman, *Theodore Dreiser: At the Gates of the City, 1871–1907* and *Theodore Dreiser: An American Journey, 1908–1945* (New York: G. P. Putnam's Sons, 1986 and 1990). Elias's emended edition of *Apostle of Nature* was published in 1970 by the Cornell University Press (Ithaca, N.Y.).
57. Tjader plays down the antipathy between herself and Helen throughout this memoir. Much of the correspondence between the two betrays their true feelings, however. Richard Lingeman rightly identifies the source of their mutual dislike when he asserts that "the two women seemed locked in a contest for Dreiser's soul." (*Theodore Dreiser: An American Journey,* 477)
58. *Twelve Men* (New York: Boni and Liveright, 1919) contained a dozen sketches of men who had made a special impression on Dreiser.
59. Nothing came of the *Culhane* project.
60. The house, which was on Cadet Court in the Hollywood hills, no longer exists, a victim of Los Angeles sprawl.
61. For the most complete record of the way in which Dreiser, with Tjader's assistance, brought the long postponed *Bulwark* project to completion, see her earlier book, *Dreiser: A New Dimension* (Norwalk, Conn.: Silvermine Press, 1965) and Jack Salzman's article "The Curious History of Dreiser's *The Bulwark*" in *Proof* 3 (1973): 21–61.
62. This fragment is not among Tjader's papers at the University of Texas, nor is it at the Dreiser collection at the University of Pennsylvania. I have quoted it directly from her manuscript.
63. Allan Hunter was born March 31, 1893, in Toronto. His father, a Scot, was then serving as minister of a large Toronto Presbyterian church.

By the time Allan Hunter reached college age, his father had moved to a ministry in Riverside, California. The junior Hunter spent a year at Occidental College cramming Greek. Subsequent theological study prepared him for summer pastorates in Canada, but service as a lieutenant in the British army interrupted his religious work. Firsthand experience of the fighting while he was stationed in Damascus altered his always ambivalent feelings about World War I and animated his interest in pacifism. After the armistice, Hunter worked briefly in an orphanage, then traveled to the Far East to study the pacifist movement. Two important influences Hunter met during his stay in India were Rabinranath Tagore and Sundar Singh. (According to Hunter's biographer, the minister did not actually meet Gandhi. Tjader's assertion to the contrary is apparently in error, perhaps signifying an inference drawn from Hunter's enthusiasm for Gandhi and the fact that he had been to India. Gandhi is one of the subjects, along with Albert Schweitzer and Toyhiko Kagawa, of Hunter's book *Three Trumpets Sound,* published by Association Press in 1939).

After his marriage to Elizabeth Walker and further study at Union Theological Seminary and Columbia University, Hunter took over the duties as pastor of the Mount Hollywood Congregational Church in 1926, a position he held until the early 1960s. During his years in Los Angeles, he developed a large following while devoting himself to a catalogue of liberal causes, including the political agenda of perennial socialist candidate Norman Thomas; opposition to racial discrimination, most notably the internment of Japanese-American citizens during World War II; and antiwar activism. Hunter retired to Claremont in 1963 with the title Pastor Emeritus. He died on July 5, 1982. Hunter was the author of some eighteen books and pamphlets as well as numerous articles that appeared in newspapers and periodicals. At the time of his brief friendship with Dreiser, Hunter was fifty-one years old.

64. While working with Dreiser on *The Bulwark,* Tjader must have been struck by the similarity between the name of the fictional Barnes estate, Thornbrough, and that of her mother's family home where Marguerite grew up. Tjader's mother's family name was Thorne and their country place was called Thorncrest.
65. Tjader's papers at the University of Texas include a memorandum and another note written by her on the circumstances surrounding the composition of "The Total Stranger," five pages of notes for the story

dictated to Tjader by Dreiser, a typed outline, and two typescripts, one marked "First typescript—carbon with Dreiser's corrections copied by MTH" and the other marked "Last typescript II with corrections copied 1945." An edited (by Thomas Riggio and Speer Morgan) version of the story was first published in *Missouri Review,* 10 (1987): 97–107.

66. Helen Dreiser did, in fact, help her husband move *The Stoic,* the third volume of the Cowperwood trilogy, almost to completion. When he died, a final chapter and a summary of the three books of the trilogy remained unfinished. Helen supplied Dreiser's notes for the final chapter in the edition posthumously published in 1947 by World.
67. This letter is quoted in its entirety as Dreiser to Harris (Tjader's married name), in Volume III of *Letters,* 1025–26.
68. *My Life With Dreiser,* 126.
69. Wilde's "Ballad of Reading Gaol" was ostensibly a memorial to Charles Thomas Wooleridge, a trooper of the Royal House Guards, and fellow inmate. Wilde had been convicted of sodomy in 1895, sentenced first to the prison at Pentonville and subsequently moved to Reading. Wooleridge was a convicted murderer. Consumed with jealousy, he had waited on the road near his house and cut his wife's throat. (Wilde's poetic license transfers the murder scene to the conjugal bed in the "Ballad.") Wooleridge's execution took place July 7, 1886. The lines to which Tjader alludes form the poem's sixth stanza and are repeated in the tenth and final stanza:

> And all men kill the thing they love,
> By all let this be heard,
> Some do it with a bitter look,
> Some with a flattering word,
> The coward does it with a kiss
> The brave man with a sword.

70. Helen was the daughter of Oregonians George and Ida Patges. She showed acting talent even as a child and longed for a theatrical career. At age sixteen she married nineteen-year-old Frank Richardson from South Carolina, an aspiring actor. They finally broke up nearly eight years later. When she met Dreiser she was a Hollywood hopeful. He was forty-seven, she twenty-five.
71. When Helen died on September 22, 1955, at age sixty-one, she left an estate of $184,380.86.
72. This essay was published in *Notes on Life,* 327–33.
73. Helen's description of Dreiser's attitude differs substantially from the

one Tjader attributes to him. In her book, Helen states that when two sets of galleys and the final typescript of *The Bulwark* got to California, Tjader was notified by phone. According to Helen, when Tjader arrived she requested that Dreiser accompany her to her house so that they could go over the galleys there. Again according to Helen, Dreiser refused and suggested that the three of them correct the galleys together in his study, whereupon an argument ensued. Dreiser won and Tjader left. (See *My Life with Dreiser,* 308). In Tjader's earlier book, she says that the phone call from Helen had indeed announced the arrival of the proofs, but that Helen claimed there was no need to worry because she had already checked them with Dreiser. According to Tjader's previous account, she rushed over to the King's Road house but was denied access to the galleys by Helen, while Dreiser stood "lost in gloomy silence." (See *Dreiser: A New Dimension,* 234–36).

74. Hilary Harris still remembers Dreiser's many kindnesses to him, especially the welcoming way the novelist opened the door for his mother and him at the King's Road house. One of the fondest memories is his serving as a young waiter for Dreiser's dinner parties attended by Charlie Chaplin, Clifford Odets, and other luminaries.

75. For a decidedly different version of this incident, see Esther McCoy's article "The Death of Dreiser" in *Grand Street* (Winter, 1988): 73–85. Esther McCoy Tobey had been an admirer of and intermittent assistant to Dreiser since before World War I. She and her husband, Berkeley Tobey, a former business manager for *Masses* during Dreiser's Greenwich Village days, were the first California friends to arrive at the King's Road house after being informed of the novelist's death. According to McCoy, she and her husband were consoling Helen when Tjader burst into the room and threw herself in a frenzy of grief onto Dreiser's body, which was being wheeled out of the house on a gurney by two ambulance attendants. Tjader then, again according to McCoy's recollection, insisted on accompanying the body in the ambulance despite the attendants' refusal based on policy. Helen's intercession finally caused the attendants to relent and the moaning Tjader was allowed to ride in the ambulance, a development McCoy attributes to Helen's remarkably objective and compassionate sense of Dreiser as a public figure. It is McCoy's version of the incident that William Lingeman accepts and incorporates in his Dreiser biography. McCoy's portrait of Tjader is uniformly negative in her essay. She accuses her of having adopted in the days of *The Bulwark* editing a "proprietary air toward Dreiser that

had finally led to her banishment from the house" (76). Like many of the women in Dreiser's life, McCoy seems to have harbored animosity toward at least one of the others who shared Dreiser's approval. But certain motives of her own may have played a role in her attitude. Elsewhere in her *Grand Street* essay, McCoy professes not to have understood why Dreiser was interested in her despite Helen's attempts to explain and notwithstanding her own testimony regarding incidents of Dreiserian sexual approaches to her. Most significantly, however, McCoy badly misjudged the novelist's relationship to Tjader. She describes an occasion from the time just before Dreiser's funeral when Tjader was pacing and brooding in the garden of the King's Road house. McCoy likens Tjader at the time to the Charlotte Brontë character Villette, "sorrowing for a love that did not bloom." (80)

Allan Hunter's biographer, Mildred Magruder, lends an additional perspective to the conflicting accounts of the scene at the novelist's death and the controversy surrounding the funeral:

> About two o'clock on the afternoon of December 27, 1945, Allan on the way to an appointment, felt, without willing it, that he must turn off Santa Monica Boulevard onto King's Road and stop at Dreiser's house. He passed the protesting Communists at the door and went directly into the bedroom, where Dreiser lay under an oxygen tent. Allan asked Mrs. Dreiser if they should have prayer, and he prayed briefly, committing everything into God's hands and to God's peace. As he left he said, "Bless you, Brother," and Dreiser recognized him with a lift of the hand. He died four hours later. Allan was asked to take the service, at the Rudyard Kilpling chapel in Forest Lawn Cemetery. John Lawson, Dorothy Healey, and other Communists were also there, and Allan felt that their intention was to conduct the service according to their own design. He resisted being overwhelmed or leaving in anger, and went ahead with the service, despite Lawson's presence. In his robe he stood at one end of the casket and Charles Chaplin at the other. Chaplin read one of Dreiser's poems, Lawson gave a criticism full of party propaganda of Dreiser as a "man of culture," and Allan spoke quietly of Dreiser's cry for compassion and his wish for the spread of power among all. He prayed, "Thou has made us all restless till we find rest in Thee." At the graveside he committed Dreiser to God. (From *Allan Armstrong Hunter,* Los Angeles: Privately Published, 1974), 171.

Also see: Thomas P. Riggio, "Dreiser's Final Hours," *Papers on Language and Literature,* vol. 27 no. 2, Spring, 1991, 300–304, which reprints Helen Dreiser's daily calendar entries for December 26, 27, and 28 of 1945; Clara Jaeger, *Philadelphia Rebel: The Education of a Bourgeoise* (London: Grosvenor, 1988), 188-190; and Ronald Baughman, "Finales: How American Writers Died; Where They're

Buried; Epitaphs and Last Words" in *American Literary Almanac,* ed. Karen L. Rood (New York: Bruccoli Clark, 1988), 338–39.

76. Dr. Vera Dreiser, a consulting and clinical psychologist and advocate of prison reform, published a not altogether complimentary book about her famous relative (*My Uncle Theodore,* Plainview, N.Y.: Nash Publishing, 1976). Lawson was an American playwright and film scenarist with leftist convictions. He had met Dreiser in the twenties when he signed on to do a subsequently aborted adaptation of *Sister Carrie.* Dreiser and Chaplin initiated their friendship in Hollywood during 1943.
77. The funeral was held on January 3, 1945, six days after Dreiser's death. By the time she wrote the manuscript of this book, Tjader apparently had forgotten the reason for the six-day hiatus between his death and his burial. The delay was caused by a Los Angeles grave-digger's strike.
78. Dreiser had a year earlier sat for a bust by Simone. The death mask became one of Tjader's most prized possessions. On the two occasions of my visits to Vikingsborg, she called my attention to it, displayed prominently in a glass case.
79. Helen's sister Myrtle became the wife of Chester Butcher shortly after Dreiser's marriage to Helen. At this writing she is still living, though confined to a nursing home.
80. Carrie Meeber is the heroine of Dreiser's *Sister Carrie* (1900). Jennie Gerhardt is the title character of his second novel, published in 1912. Roberta Alden is the unfortunate drowning victim in *An American Tragedy,* played on the screen by Sylvia Sidney in the 1931 movie of the same name and by Shelley Winters in the 1951 adaptation of the book, *A Place in the Sun. A Gallery of Women,* published by Liveright in 1929, sketches fifteen real-life women Dreiser had known. The book makes a companion piece to his *Twelve Men.*
81. *Hey-Rub-a-Dub-Dub* was a sometimes incoherent and intemperate collection of philosophical essays published by Boni and Liveright in 1920.
82. Powys's letter to Helen is missing from the University of Pennsylvania's Dreiser Collection. I have quoted it exactly from Tjader's manuscript.
83. The young scholar was Sydney Horowitz. He had written his doctoral dissertation on the novelist. (*Theodore Dreiser: Basic Patterns of His Work,* University of Pittsburgh,1951). During the winter of 1953, with the help of a grant, Horowitz worked at organizing Dreiser's *Notes* but became ill in March and died on July 6. As opposed to Tjader's view of Horowitz's methodology, Neda Westlake, longtime custodian of

Dreiser's papers at the University of Pennsylvania, believes that Horowitz's sorting out of secondary sources and arranging the *Notes* manuscript was "consistent with Dreiser's outline" and "convincing proof" of the scholar's "editorial competence and grasp of Dreiser's methods of work." See Westlake, "Dreiser's Notes on Life," *University of Pennsylvania Library Chronicle,* XX, 1954, 69–75.

84. Compton was a University of Chicago physicist whose discoveries included the change in wave length of scattered X rays (known as the Compton effect), and the total reflection of X rays. The Compton effect won him the Nobel Prize for physics in 1927. Dreiser had met Compton in 1935 while the novelist was lecturing in Chicago.
85. Jesuit priest, biologist, and theologian Pierre Teilhard de Chardin is best known in America for two books, *The Phenomenon of Man* (1955) and *The Divine Milieu* (1957). Both attempt to bring science and religion together by positing that man is evolving toward godhead. Several similarities between Dreiser's late ideas and those of the Frenchman were pointed out in my book about the novelist. See *Dreiser and His Fiction: A Twentieth-Century Quest* (Philadelphia: University of Pennsylvania Press, 1983), 186–87.
86. *Notes on Life,* 80–81
87. Ibid, 279.

Appendix A

Original Introduction by Marguerite Tjader (1976)

Dreiser was a figure baffling to many in his generation. As I look back, certain qualities of his persist and grow clearer in perspective. Who is going to signal them as the number of those who knew him grows smaller?

Dreiser's image has often been distorted by critics, kicked around by lesser personalities who did not understand him, nor his way of writing and thinking. He has been called a liar, a bad writer, a woman-chaser, and some have maligned him without honesty or taste. Still more distressing is the total ignorance of Dreiser shown by many younger people today. Some schools skip over his work with scarcely a comment. We can only refer them to manuals on American Literature (or give them a short entry from the *Encyclopedia* here). Yet even to many who know him and acknowledge his greatness, he was an enigma.

There has been much discussion about Dreiser's attitudes toward sex and marriage, which were once considered scandalous, but pale beside what is written today. Yet no one has tried to understand his philosophy of love nor have many read his philosophy of life as it developed over a period of more that thirty years, and finally was published as *Notes on Life* (University of Alabama Press, 1970).

Since I was privileged to have worked with Dreiser at several different periods, I feel compelled to add to his record, as a still-living witness to his essential qualities. As his work belongs to the future, so does his stature as a man. I am willing to share my experience of knowing him and many of his friends, and to speak of him because of the confidence he showed in his letters to me. These, and certain unpublished materials from his files, as well as photographs, make up this manuscript.

Because of his extraordinary frankness in discussing his own emotions and his ability to describe those of the characters of whom he writes, Dreiser offers a unique opportunity to study the psychology of sex as he so well understood it. In his philosophy of love there are no pornographic details but only a great poetry of the senses, a mystique of love and a great longing for continuity, something beyond the deep human agonies and joys in which he so fully participated.

We should not forget, however, that love of work, above all, was his central drive. Ever diligent, he forced himself to the task at hand, no matter how tired he felt, discouraged or depressed. "I go out so little," he wrote to me once, "heaven for me should consist of a desk and a window and a chair—afloat in space." But because beyond his work he was himself exceptional, the psycho-neurotic, the artist, the mystic, the sensualist, the wildly passionate saint or devil—all of these categories might apply to him, though none fit him exactly—he interested the public as a man.

In the last decades, there have been gradual shifts of values in both political and philosophical fields. Fixed theories have been shaken, rethought because of an increasingly holistic view of man's behavior and destiny.

Orthodoxy in politics or religion is moderating; Marxism is challenged by Euro-Communism; many varieties of socialism are being worked out. Human rights issues are creating a new political criterion.

The Catholic church, since Vatican II, has undergone its own revolution in the practice of social ideals—(According to a recent article on South America, in the *New York Times,* many young priests have been denounced as socialists)!

Religions in general are seeking a common ground in good works, and in the practice of prayer and meditation. Some have gone back to early Biblical practices, emotional singing, healing, "speaking in tongues."

Mystical experiences have emerged from the secrecy of the monastery. People are seeking contact with the supernatural on every level, trying to understand spiritual ecstasy and even demonic possession.

In all these fields, Dreiser was ahead of his time. He invented his own political stance, cutting across lines and theories, to express his ideas of equity and the need for social betterment.

Dreiser had delved into psychological studies and also investigated various religions. He would have been interested to see that today, priests are sent to study psychology, to be able to help their parishioners, and psychiatrists are acknowledging that religion, as explained by Carl Jung, plays a crucial part in many lives. (A certain Dr. Bollinger of the Menninger Foundation, said lately: "Now there is a genuine two-way exchange; it is just as important to know what religion can offer, as what psychiatry can.") But Dreiser had always taken from established forms of thought, whatever he wanted to use in his own life-picture.

He had studied Oriental religions, and quotes from the Chinese philosophers as well as from the Vedantists. After his immersion in Quaker writings, while working on *The Bulwark,* he stated that if he wanted to adopt any one religion, it would be that of the Friends, with their emphasis on justice and the Inner Light.

In his later years, Dreiser began to develop his own cosmology based on his unique study of science and nature and the Creative Force which he felt was driving him.

In seeking to penetrate into the spiritual essence of life, he approached the intuitions of the now-famed philosopher Teilhard de Chardin, whose work was not yet published in Dreiser's time. The articulate Frenchman sensed even in rocks and stones, a "spiritual envelope," which was the first manifestation of an inner development in sensate creatures, and finally in man, of a soul, the sign or seat of a divine Spirit.

Dreiser, in his more fumbling way, attributed life in mysterious measure to the whole universe, as it is animated an directed by an inscrutable Force, or Energy.

The term bioenergy is used today to try to define and study a certain subtle, but sometimes measurable force which can be emitted from the vitality of a person, affecting others as love, hate, healing power, or causing telepathy, attraction. Dreiser did not use this word, but this force was very real to him, coming from person to person, or perhaps streaming through the universe, to be picked up by sensitive souls. Dreiser used the word love, in this new sense, as indeed, today, it is used in double, triple meanings. It is used as concern for the handicapped, for prisoners, for civil rights victims, expressions that have become symbols for the increasing compassion which is stirring in the world today, in the face of poverty, crime, violence, or despair. This theme is brought out clearly in *The Bulwark;* the need of love, as the need for food, can explain much of man's misery.

In his *Notes on Life,* Dreiser goes further into the exploration of man's life-force, given and received. The power and beauty of Nature is everywhere brought out, and the overall Mechanism of the universe is sensed, if not fully understood, operating in order and harmony, in spite of great contrasts and balances. Or perhaps because of these very contrasts and balances, harmony is maintained. The essential unity of all things becomes increasingly apparent.

The time has come to reassess Dreiser in a new, prophetic role. Lover of mankind, as he has always been, he sees into the future as Blake did in his day, and looks for the development of man, perhaps not in his own strength, but because of the Creative Force coming through him.

Dreiser is still ahead of his time. It is essential to an understanding of him, to see how he anticipated the spiritual trends and expanding concepts of our days.

Appendix B

Dreiser's Contributions to *Direction* Magazine

December 1937
"Introduction" (To the First Issue)

As the antique order of an old house becomes the disorderly decay of a newer age, so with changing ideas. The refreshing tides of seasons, years and generations succeed each other, not without sadness and despair and suffering for what was, but mainly with welcome and gladness for the vitality and promise of what will be. To some it is necessary to find out these new directions, build new forms, be the van of circumstance; and to some is necessary blindness and sterility of age and decay. This balance is part of the universe of which our puny ideas, theories, and proclamations are only a reflection, but a necessity, or so it seems. The seeming of what is new is only possible through the seeming of the old. The eager delight of a fall wind takes its rise from the ennui of summer heat. And who does not thrill to the arrival of what is untried and promising power and delight?

January, 1938
"Theodore Dreiser & John Dos Passos: A Conversation"

Time: December 17, 1937
Place: Dreiser's Apartment, New York City

Dreiser: What do you think of Roosevelt, and the Republican party, and this new labor party? What have you heard or felt, or think, would be the drift of things now? In two years we're going to have another shake-up. This Labor government we have had has something behind it, and it has a good man. I mean, LaGuardia will make a good man. Do you think they will take him?

Dos Passos: I think things are pointing toward LaGuardia. You can't tell whether he will jump with the remnants of the Republican party, plus the Left Democrats—the liberal Democrats, or whether the liberal Democrats will be the nucleus of a new party.

Dreiser: Do you know whether this new Labor party, the American Labor party, feels that LaGuardia is really the ideal man for them, or are they just waiting for someone?

Dos Passos: I think they're pretty suspicious of LaGuardia. At the same time, he is very energetic.

Dreiser: And he is honest. He doesn't trim anybody financially, and he does want to improve social conditions.

Dos Passos: Like all politicians, he has made some awful compromises, like the endorsement of Harvey in Queens.

Dreiser: According to the *Times* this morning, there was something of a Labor convention where Lewis was, and somebody got up and asked whether he would accept the nomination for president on the Labor ticket. But he was just going out the door and he escaped. Do you think that if Lewis headed a Labor ticket, that would be good for the radical side?

Dos Passos: I wouldn't say that it would. I think there is too much opposition to Lewis. I think Detroit was a poor move. The C.I.O. got a beating there.

Dreiser: Well, apart from Lewis and LaGuardia, there isn't anybody, is there?

Dos Passos: No, unless the Democratic party can bring up Wallace.

Dreiser: Well, I was just going to say that Wallace was a possibility.

Dos Passos: The question with LaGuardia would be an interesting one. I am very anxious to get out to the Middle West, because people who have been out to Kansas say that the farmer's opposition to the C.I.O. is very strong.

Dreiser: How is it toward Roosevelt?

Dos Passos: Roosevelt is still riding high. He has lost some, but not much.

Dreiser: Lewis couldn't get in?

Dos Passos: Yes, but I don't think he could be disinfected in two years.

Dreiser: I just wonder whether there is anybody at all that could take these various liberal parties and weld them and get somewhere. I thought at one time that Roosevelt was grooming his son, but he hasn't got much time to show whether he is really marvelous or not.

Dos Passos: James is more likely to try something in Massachusetts politics first. I think that's his plan.

Dreiser: And I suppose the South would split off completely from any radical Labor party?

Dos Passos: I'm not sure. What do you think of it? They re-elected Maverick. There was a lot of money spent trying to throw him out but they re-elected him.

Dreiser: I don't think the cotton industries would favor any labor group.

Dos Passos: Oh, no, they couldn't, and down there the chance of insurrection among the parties is pretty thin. They'd get more people in Texas and Oklahoma than in the Black Belt.

Dreiser: Another thing. I wonder how much reactionary politics is being fostered by money, and whether it could be put over. There are a number of people who like to play the Fascist game, like Hague and Hoffman over here in New Jersey for example—pure Fascist. And throughout the country there are others.

Dos Passos: McNutt in Indiana.

Dreiser: Is he another?

Dos Passos: Yes, with very fancy trimmings. He has a great Legion following, as he was General Commander.

Dreiser: I thought he was more liberal than that.

Dos Passos: He said a good thing—that if Fascism ever triumphed in this country, it would be under the name of Anti-Fascism.

Dreiser: I believe that's true.

Dos Passos: It would have to be somebody with a lot of sugar in him.

Dreiser: It seems to me that there is an awful lot of stirring. I get evidence of it every day in the mails, from all kinds of people that have an idea that something can be done in some particular way in their region. Or that their region should be the head and front of some new lineup that would bring this country into—well, not a radical, but a democratic, anti-capitalist set-up—like for instance, that of Upton Sinclair, if he can get enough support for his cooperative group to be allowed to take land.

Dos Passos: That's a further development of the E.P.I.C. plan.

Dreiser: I think that working along these lines might really swing things around, because you know we have had that community idea in this country for a long time. I mean in Brook Farm and Oneida and Harmony, and Germantown, and with the Mennonites, where there were people who were ready to start right in on something they thought was worthwhile.

Dos Passos: Some of those communities have been successful too for long periods. The descendants of the Oneida Community get Dividends from it. It has become quite a wealthy enterprise. I have known several people who have had, not large, but small incomes from the Oneida Community, because their mothers or fathers were in it.

Dreiser: Yes, there are great returns on honest Communist farming.

Dos Passos: It's very funny, but when it works, it makes money.

Dreiser: Sinclair's idea is really in line with that, but doesn't have the underlying religious basis that moved the other people. Religion certainly moved the Quakers. Their's is a communal religion. Then, too, it was outside the line of outside economic interests. But Sinclair's idea is really the same, only on a much larger scale, you know. But I don't know what would drive this country into it. Extreme economic necessity might do it. On the other hand, if people are truly dissatisfied with the capitalistic set-up, it might not require economic disaster. They might just like the idea. But Sinclair argues this all the time. He devotes a lot of space to it every week. He is getting a lot of applause on it.

Dos Passos: I still believe that practically all this started with people on relief.

Dreiser: Yes, to a certain extent, only his argument now is that people who want to save money, who are burdened with rents, high cost of living, education, etc., could do much better for themselves if they would just get a grant of land somewhere—a grant from the government, and start a little community, or a large one, which should be tolerated in the United States.

Dos Passos: Yes.

Dreiser: Well, to me, that is one thing which might be done. If this capitalistic crowd got too argumentative or too bothersome, people might try it. What I thought was that maybe a Government provision for such a thing might be injected into a party platform.

Dos Passos: It is interesting to talk to people on W.P.A. projects. A great many hate to go back to private industry. Although they don't make very much in working for the government, there is great enthusiasm on these projects. The W.P.A. writers, people who have been working on this guide book, are all people who are really ineligible. They really can't make the grade in the struggle for money. And they are much happier. They would rather take less and live easier. They feel that they can't face the terrible competition in private industry.

Dreiser: Most people really think that is a good, a swell argument for a party. They won't have to work so hard.

Dos Passos: Well, of course the type of work it takes to make money isn't the same as production. Making money is a separate art, by itself. I think the state mind of this country has changed. Five years ago, a great many Americans pretended to be very hopeful about what happened in Russia. I think now because of the terrific terror, because of the fact that the terror has to keep on, and keeps going on, people feel that something is not working there.

Dreiser: Well, I was strong for Russia and for Stalin and the whole program, but in the last year, I have begun to think that maybe it won't be better than anything else.

Dos Passos: Well, though, look at the achievements of the French Revolution, a great many survived through the period following Napoleon. I think a great many of its achievements are still going on.

Dreiser: Yes, and a great many achievements of the Russian Revolution are right here with us. We're indebted to them for a lot of things—40 hour week, W.P.A.—I mean for public works—the dole, because they had the dole over there from the first. Wages and laws, control of farming. This bill that's up now. That would never have come in this country except for Russia and 1917, at least not in our day.

Dos Passos: No. I think all the great achievements of the Russian Revolution have been made, and have been absorbed into history. And I still don't understand what's happening there. It sounds like . . .

Dreiser: And damned if I do. They claim they give the Russians a liberal education, you know, a technical education from farming and dairying up. They also give them training in the arts, the natural approach to the arts, pertaining to the theater, the libraries, and gymnastics, health, diet—all of that is supposed to go with being a Russian. But what seems to be lacking is the question of ideology, of what they are to think. And they are to think that any other form of government is insane and that everybody outside of Russia is worse off than they are, that they are less miserable than anybody else. I know that for a fact. Still, that may be a temporary condition, an attempt to achieve cohesion and unity. It has been how many years now? Twenty years, and they have done that much, but it's just a question in my mind whether they'll do more, or whether Russia will be liberalized. Maybe they want to have a little religion, or greater class differences, or a little more money—less standardization in life, you know.

Dos Passos: Yes.

Dreiser: I don't really think that question can be settled for another five years, or ten.

Dos Passos: It is very hard to tell now, though the general impression you get from impartial observers—who are very hard to get—people like Victor Sayre [*sic*].

Dreiser: I don't think there is such a thing as an impartial observer.

Dos Passos: Yes, of course. A lot of people claim that this present privileged bureaucracy has been built up. . . .

Dreiser: On the other hand, there's Japan, looking toward a dictatorial and so an imperialized world, with the problem of means as the first bet—it's bound to have an effect on the thinking of this country. These various situations. I think everybody must be thinking of how this country is going, and what it ought to be like.

Dos Passos: Yes, everybody, except the dyed-in-the-wool conservatives who seem not to be thinking at all. They just seem to be going into a hysteria. You can't get anywhere in talking to fanatic Communists, or the fanatic element of the Capitalists, both of whom talk as if things were about twenty-five years ago.

Dreiser: Supposing a person could achieve a new set-up here, what do you think it ought to be like? Now here we are. It could go, according to the difficulties, in different directions, you know. It could go toward fascism or toward Communism, or some intermediate state. Assuming that it could go in any direction, what should the country do? Go how far? Abolish capitalism completely?

Dos Passos: I don't think so.

Dreiser: Would you Russianize this country if you could?

Dos Passos: No, it would be better to get the basic industries and monopolies under some kind of public control.

Dreiser: How much public control?

Dos Passos: Under complete public control. But, of course, to do that, you have got to invent a technique by which industry can be run democratically. You have got to find some kind of spirit for that. Get the New England town meeting into bureaucratic industry in some form.

Dreiser: Suppose you can't find that. You're sunk. You need an ideal for doing so. Some kind of American religion. You would have to have people believe, like the Quakers, that there is a certain almost spiritual relationship which should be maintained—not too much money, and not too much liberty for anybody.

Dos Passos: Yes.

Dreiser: But I am not too sure at what point in this you put your foot down on industrialists with a bang.

Dos Passos: You do on the economic line.

Dreiser: Wouldn't you be doing it on a creative—I don't mean exactly intellectually creative, and I don't mean commercial creativeness, I mean technically creative—wouldn't you be putting your foot down on a possible very great scientific or technical development which would require extreme individuality?

Dos Passos: I don't think it would, so much as a kind of balance between individuals.

Dreiser: If we had a school system that was carefully worked out, it would act the same as a religion. But still, if we had a school system or educational program that was carefully calculated to give your brother a square deal and to see that the square pegs were fitted into the square holes according to their talents, etc., no such thing as too much wealth or abject poverty—and if you had in addition a program that put the idea over and maintained it—well, would that be all right?

Dos Passos: It would be a part of right. It wouldn't mean anything unless it was hitched to a form of society that allowed people to live that way. The present form of capitalism in America is a definite brake on useful work, because making money and doing useful work have less and less connection. Making money is a special art in handling the system. I think taking a profit is a special art. I don't know that actually making money is such an evil thing as taking a profit from labor.

Dreiser: Money-making in a big way is always like that. To do it, people need a vast financial backing.

Dos Passos: I think the right way in education is to watch it for the idea—an educational system to make you feel that a social relationship was the relationship, and that any variation from that was something very bad. A fixed educational system is a social ideal which isn't too much or too little of anything. They have tried to do that in Russia.

Dreiser: I haven't been there for a long time—I was there in '28, almost ten years ago, and all the kids seemed to feel that profit was a disgraceful thing, much like people would think of house-breaking here. Would you say that the literature and the press of the country should be held to the support of such a program, or would you give them a free rein to say all they pleased?

Dos Passos: I would give them free rein.

Dreiser: In that case would you be sure that the whole thing wouldn't be suddenly disorganized by outside comment and that the whole ideological system wouldn't be destroyed?

Dos Passos: It would have to take its chance, if you didn't turn out a good enough system of society it would crash. A good system should run of itself.

Dreiser: You would keep a free press, with the privilege of any form of comment or denunciation? You might have a book like *Looking Backward,* only looking forward to some state in which the "real people" would have the dough and be happy, and the dunce left in the ashcan. That is possible in what you call the free press. You would take the chance?

Dos Passos: I certainly would. If your system of society averaged up to anything for people such a breakdown wouldn't happen.

Dreiser: What would you do about religion?

Dos Passos: No religion—at any rate, in such a state, a religious body couldn't exist as a corporation.

Dreiser: You wouldn't let them hold property? You would have no religious education, no religious property? Would you allow them to collect money?

Dos Passos: Well, I think you would have to tax them or something. The best thing that could happen in this country would be taxes on religious property. It's value is going up by leaps and bounds.

Dreiser: In view of the scientific trend of the day, would you tolerate any form of religion, or would you try, as Hitler does, to organize some theory of life that people could have reverence for, or a certain amount of it to influence the people in the general direction of your educational system?

Dos Passos: Once religious foundations are thoroughly taxed, there wouldn't be any trouble.

Dreiser: Do you really think some sane attitude of reverence for the human race would come about of its own accord under your system?

Dos Passos: I think it would be better than the present.

Dreiser: You wouldn't establish any religion, say on the basis of present-day science?

Dos Passos: I think to produce such a social turnover, you would have to have a tremendous body of emotional feeling, but I think if it got to be a religion, it would turn out to be a racket, like every other religion.

Dreiser: The Quaker sect didn't turn out to be a racket.

Dos Passos: Practically the only one which never did. For one thing, there is no money in it.

Dreiser: That's just the point. How much understanding of life would go with this education system? Not all people are going to believe that because the laws are fair and the Constitution reads right, that it's going to be that way.

Dos Passos: No.

Dreiser: And then there is your press—perfectly free to say what it pleases, and its all right if these people establish a religion. You wouldn't do anything about safeguarding the thing? You would just go that far and then just let it run?

Dos Passos: If it didn't run on its own momentum, it wouldn't be any use, but it couldn't fall right back. The human system is changing all the time.

Dreiser: Do you really believe that? You believe that the world is approaching a more humane attitude[?].

Dos Passos: No doubt that various social forms of organization are continually evolving. Of course, how much you could do with them is the question. The set-up has gotten worse since the war. You can see a definite lowering of human values all over the world.

Dreiser: Well, what makes you hope that any such state—any equitable state is going to evolve?

Dos Passos: It's all in relative terms.

Dreiser: You think it is going to evolve?

Dos Passos: We have a better chance in America.

Dreiser: In the countries I have been in, I'll be damned if I have seen it evolve for the common man at all. Common people's lives here are just about the same as under the Kaiser and in England; the details are pathetic.

Dos Passos: Just the same, America is probably the country where the average guy has got the better break. Any system, however good, would tend to decay. The main question for people at present is to have things not get worse.

Dreiser: Do you think we're doing a pretty good job? Do you think America right now is doing very poorly or pretty well?

Dos Passos: It seemed to me this time coming home that there was more chance for people in America, and the people looked livelier, better. I think the chance of its getting much worse very bad. As the financial system gets more uneasy, it will lead to its own decay. We have got to start with what we've got. We can't invent something.

Dreiser: I think the moment you try to nail things down, you are liable to get nowhere.

Dos Passos: I was more or less convinced—well not completely—but was willing to give the Russians the benefit of the doubt for a number of years. But I think, as you say, that what goes on in Russia, the result of trying to nail things down, are not very good.

Dreiser: Well, so far it certainly looks that way. I was just wondering. You work with a theory of fair play—and then of course you either bolster that by an educational system, you know, and a proper attitude, not free opinion, but with something stronger to keep blood in it, you know—or, you let it drift and anything can happen. That's why I was so interested in the question of religion and the press, as to what really follows a turnover. If you could feel that such a thing naturally appealed to what you call the human spirit, and that people would instinctively choose your system—but it doesn't look as if they do that. There is always something that comes up and upsets the cart.

Dos Passos: There has really never been any set-up in the Western world, up to the present American set-up, where it would be possible to produce enough goods without a slave class, and I think now that new techniques are getting us to the point where it is possible. I think a sensible government would take over industries and compensate the present owners, and then deflate the money afterwards. Finance has reached a point where a government can use slight of hand just like anybody else.

Dreiser: Yes, like the Indian-giver. Run around the corner and take it away on thc other side.

Dos Passos: Well, every time there is a rise in wages, prices go up at the A&P!

September-October 1938
"Equity between Nations"

(This speech was made by Dreiser in Paris at a conference to which he was invited by an international group headed by Lord Cecil of England and Georges Bonnet, Finance Minister of France.)

The work of two American Committees, that asked me to come here as one of their representatives, is really aimed to abolish war and establish democracy. The phrases "peace and democracy" and "against war and fascism" actually includes [*sic*] the hope of stopping the bombardment of innocent civilians, whether they be women and children or unarmed workers or merchants or professionals in whatever fields they may be. At bottom the campaign is for fair play or legal conduct between antagonists, however just or unjust their antagonisms may be. To this end the committees I represent seek to arouse favorable public sentiment the world over.

This particular conference, as I understand it, has been called to devise ways and means of doing all of these things. Some people, like Mr. Blum in France and Lord Halifax in England and our own Secretary of State, Mr. Hull, are wondering, how for instance, Italy and Germany and Spain, the loyalists and the rebels, the Chinese and Japanese can be harmonized. How to initiate mediation between them, to get them not to do the things they are doing.

Only the other day, when the King was here, your premier, Mr. Daladier, your ex-premier Mr. Blum, Mr. Herriot, your president of the Chamber, and Lord Halifax agreed sadly, that mediation could be undertaken only by the five Great Powers. By them, I assume, they mean: Germany, Italy, France, England and Russia (if they are willing to concede that Russia is a Great Power), or possibly, as someone said, by England single-handed. I don't suppose, in view of the present attitude of the United States, that they feel that they can.

However, I can tell you, a real majority of the American people would like to see their government do something about all this. And it is actually the work of the League of American Writers and the American League against War and Fascism, to persuade the people of America to compel their government to do this. And they are certainly making progress. Public sentiment against dishonest and unjustified war and oppression is very strong in America. It is not as strong as it was in the days of slavery or when Royal Spain was oppressing Cuba, but it can well become so.

In England, if I read the events in that country correctly, there is now developing among the English masses an opinion which may, and I hope will, force the responsible executives of that government to be less soft spoken about which they have done little or nothing. That I am right as to this, seems to me to be confirmed by that meeting here in Paris that I was just talking about. Because there Lord Halifax told his French questioners, that the bombardment of open towns in Spain and China had deeply moved public opinion in England. But he also said, that it was no easy matter to reform.

It will never be an easy matter. And fair play will not come between nations, until fair play between capital and labour in the various nationalities has been established. Nor will it come, until the majority of individuals of all lands and nationalities stop pinning their faith to wealth, and by that I mean individual wealth as against national wealth, as the only way to secure for them, individually, comfort and safety. For individual wealth leads to the grouping or union of the possessors of such wealth as against those who have not so much, in order that they may retain it, regardless of all others. And this leads directly to those class hatreds that divide and weaken nations internally and—externally—to cause them to war on other nations which have more than they have or which seek or seem to seek (as they think) to prevent them from obtaining what they desire. In other words, as nations, it leads to internal and external quarreling, injustice and inhuman wars such as we see today.

But when any one says that, the individual replies: "Well, that is all right. But if I don't take care of myself, no one else will." And until men of good will and good sense the world over sit down together and think out ways and means of making their governments deal fairly between the strong and the weak, the intelligent and the unintelligent, the cunning and the innocent, he will certainly struggle to take care of himself in any way that he can, honestly or dishonestly. The masses, and by that I mean all the individuals of the masses, must learn, that they can only expect a fair reward for what they do if they insist and see too it, that every other individual receives a fair reward for what he does.

In America we say: "fifty-fifty" and the masses really want our representatives and our executives to see that this "fifty-fifty" is secured to all. Our constitution calls for it and our present president, Mr. Roosevelt, is quite cautiously trying to bring it about by democratic means. However, there as everywhere else in the world, he has the strong and the greedy and the lazy and the vain, who happen to have the majority of the wealth of the country, or would like to have it, to deal with.

These do not want fair play as between them and the man who has little or nothing. They insist on trying to be giants in a world that consists only of little men, for certainly we are all of us little men, and we have not yet solved exactly how to establish equity. But when we begin trying, you will not have England seizing India, Italy Abyssinia, Japan China, the United States the Panama Canal, as it did at first, but you will have an effort to bring the means of subsistence and the opportunity of self-development to every individual the world over. And when you have that, you will not have a world in which men are almost compelled to seize each other by the throat in order to live. But my feeling at this time is that, if a Great World War can be avoided, it is entirely possible that some world conference, such as this one would like to be, will bring about a plan, that may help all nations to avoid this old cut throat individualism. And for this reason this particular world conference—because of the thought and the feeling for men of all nations that prompts it—has enormous significance for me.

This hall is small, the number of people here is not many, but the word that could go out from here, might be so wise, so valuable, that it would move millions of people. For what I read and hear in many places today, leads me to believe, that many many people are weary, and more than that, disgusted with this silly struggle for enormous individual wealth and enormous individual power. For, as you can see for yourself, these things can no longer mean really anything in a world, where millions realize, that no man anywhere is so very different from any other and where they are beginning to see, that to do the really great things in life, the good things, the helpful things, the beautiful things the individual does not need great wealth, nor great power. Today, neither great wealth, nor great power can rest in the hands of any single individual. Because no individual can possibly wisely handle all of the things which great wealth and great power demand of him. He must have help. He must have the information, which has never yet resided in any one individual and never will.

Wisdom and knowledge exist only in the minds of all of the people—not in those of just a few. You may know medicine, I don't. And millions of other people don't either. You may know engineering, or law, or surgery, or chemistry. I don't. Probably not a man or a woman in this room knows much more than a little of any of these things. But in all of the minds of all of the people of the world today, including as these do, all of the knowledge that has been gathered by their ancestors and worked out in the form of habits, customs, implements, materials, machines, architecture, art and the books that describe these things, are to be found the knowledge and the wisdom by which we live or seek to. So that no one man anywhere nor any single nation anywhere can claim to know all, or how to arrange life for everybody, everywhere. Besides there is too much to be known. We have yet to learn and we must be humble and co-operative in the search.

And for that reason individual vanity and individual greed leading as these often do (through the vainglorious and the greedy groups they evoke), to national vanities and national greeds must be curbed. For these provoke international hatred and wars and so injure man as a whole—stop his progress—wipe out his achievements as they frequently do.

So let me repeat, that since most of the knowledge of today is not even in nations' individuals but in books written by dead men, piled up in libraries or laboratories and willed by them to us without charge, we must not expect or want too much individually. This building, this city, all of the processes by which we live, by which this nation lives and any other nation lives, was willed by other generations to this generation. You did not pay for this street outside any more than you paid for the Atlantic Ocean. You found it here. It was given to you. And no one should be charged too much for what was already here, when he came. That is why I feel that more fair play must come into life. We are—all of us—co-heirs of all that is. We should find ways and means of sharing peacefully what has been given to us by nature and other men, without fighting, without bombing cities, without murdering women and children and people, who do not want unjustly to take anything from anyone.

I hope, that this world Conference will be able, to make a few suggestions, which may appeal to the individuals of all nations and more, move them to endeavour [sic] to work this out.

November-December 1938
"Barcelona in August"

We felt war immediately as we crossed the border of Spain in an old car, and sped toward Barcelona. A sense of impending catastrophe difficult to define at first. Spain is beautiful. The air, the color, the little farms, many unchanged in appearance, have great charm. But everything is infected by fear. A flight of birds may startle you as if it were an air raid. In all the little villages, the central squares or market places are cut across by deep trenches into which people may throw themselves at the sound of the siren announcing airplanes. As we near Barcelona, shell-shattered homes and villages grow more frequent. I saw one village cut literally in half by a shell. One part standing and with people going about their business. The other smashed, wiped out, dead. Then several villages I saw were completely shattered, annihilated. Little villages, without any possible military significance. In these, most of the people were gone. But there were usually a few old ones, sitting in the ruins of their homes, cooking, even, between broken walls. In a certain village I saw only one old woman, sitting in a dream of misery.

Barcelona is a beautiful city. It is one of the fine cities of the world. I wish I could describe its charm beside the sea. It has great modern buildings, great powerful docks. Many have been destroyed, but it is still a magnificent city.

But five miles of serpentine subways cut under the city. They have built them irregularly, with openings at all sorts of unexpected spots, with several entrances at all central places. They have built them like rabbits' burrows, so that if one entrance or exit is blocked, they can escape by another. The passages are very clever and very deep. There is room for benches, in some places. In others real shelters, with running water, lights, have been prepared. Some people spend half the day in these places, when an air raid has been announced. Big sirens have usually time to announce a raid five minutes before the bombs can drop. Sometimes they keep screeching off and on for a whole day. There have been several three-day raids, when planes kept coming over the city again and again, not always to drop bombs, but to terrorize.

The hotel at which I stayed was a big handsome structure, in the most luxurious European style. Its kitchen had been carried partly away by a bomb. But business went on as usual. In the dining room, waiters served on silver platters—one bun and the black juice they call coffee. There is no meat, no sugar, no butter, no milk. They serve a sort of pap, made out of vegetable matter. It is nourishing, to some extent, and fried with sauce, vaguely resembles meat. The heavy furniture and hangings are still there. But there are no sheets on the beds. All available linen or fine cloth has been taken for bandages for the wounded. There is no soap. In the whole of Barcelona, you cannot buy a piece of soap. When I had been there a few days, I developed an itch on my neck and cheek. I could get no soap nor ointment. At the drugstore, I was given a sort of herb, which had no effect on my neck whatsoever. I was told that all ointments or antiseptics were needed for the wounded. And over a third of the inhabitants of Barcelona are suffering the "itch" without any way of treating it. (It was only two weeks after I got back to Paris that I got rid of mine!)

The clothes of the people show what they endure. The clothes of the middle-class people are now as miserable as those of the poor. Their shoes are worn out, broken open, tied with strings. They go about on foot. Since one of the big power plants was destroyed, there are no street lights and no street cars. A few official cars are the only means of getting about. Most horses and donkeys have disappeared. In the morning, you see little groups of people setting out on foot with sacks. They go out to forage in the country around Barcelona. They come back in the evening with a few sticks of fire wood, a cabbage, or a few turnips, etc., or with nothing at all. There are twelve million Loyalists in territory which before held about two million. They are slowly starving.

Suffering has brought out a marvelous spirit in the people which is stronger than anything you can imagine. I spoke to Del Vayo and Negrin. Del Vayo is a stocky, honest man in civilian clothes. Negrin, too, wears civilian clothes. They impress you as intellectuals rather than politicians. They said they had, in certain black moments, considered giving in, to save the people more suffering. But they were convinced that the people themselves would not give in. They would rather get new leaders and go on. Del Vayo said they can go on fighting for a year, and a half.

Such spirit as there is in Spain seems to me—well—beautiful.

Of course Hitler and Mussolini are backing Franco, but not to the extent that he had hoped. On the other hand, France and Russia have not been helping the Loyalists nearly as much as has been thought. When I first arrived in Paris to attend the conference called by Bonnet of France and Lord Cecil of England, against the Bombing of Open Cities, I was greatly surprised to find that the conference was a sort of diplomatic manoeuvre [*sic*] to reconcile other nations to England's attitude of Hands-off—the making of humanitarian phrases without humanitarian aims. In some measure, this prepared me for the attitude of Chamberlain and Daladier in the Czechoslovakian crisis. This indifference of certain powerful individuals representing England and France, to the fate of the Spanish government. A protest was voiced against Hitler's treatment of Catholics, but no protest against Franco or Mussolini's bombing of the Open Cities was allowed. The Appasionara, famous Loyalist woman envoy, was not allowed to speak. When they learned of my views on Spain at a luncheon just before I was to speak, they did everything to put my speech off, and only at the end of the session, as I still sat on the platform, were they obliged to call on me. (This speech was printed in *Direction* last month.) The next day, I spoke at a French Writers Congress which showed the true spirit of the French people toward Spain. But this spirit of sympathy and would-be cooperation, is everywhere blocked by those in authority. The Loyalists have large sums of money in the banks of Paris, which belong to the government of Spain. But since Franco also claims these funds, financial powers have been able to keep them tied up "till the end of the war." The Loyalists need them desperately now, but are not even allowed credit against them. When I left Barcelona, I told Del Vayo I would telephone the French minister Bonnet to ask if he could send a few automobiles, urgently needed for transportation across the border. But nothing was done, at least during the remaining two weeks of my stay in Europe.

January 1939
"Dreiser Answers French Labor"

(Telegram sent to Messidor, official organ of the C.G.T. Federation of all French Labor Unions, in answer to request for his support in recent crisis.)

"I am not ready to believe that France of the Revolution and the 1848 uprising and the great war is a France that will be dominated by a dictator who would make Fascist robots of Frenchmen.

"If the workers, even to a fraction of their real number, were to rise and defy this financial group that wishes to subordinate and enslave them they would win. It seems to me that the heroic struggle of their neighbor friends, the Loyalists of Spain should inspire them to fight. If so, these two high democratic causes might win together, and it is my hope that they will do so."

May-June 1939
"To the Third Annual Congress" (of the League of American Writers)

The writer, artist, poet, musician has truly an appointment with life in the large—himself, society, the earth, the universe. But most of all with the individual called himself as related to these others, and as the medium through which, according to his temperament, these others are to be represented to others. It follows that his concern with writers as writers is secondary although it does not follow that collectively as well as individually they may not meet to further and protect the particular social arrangements and environments which make their arts, as well as the arts and lives of others, possible. And in times of social change and stress it is historic that the artist in every field, but especially the writer, has voiced most of society's deepest needs—its ills and its highest aspirations. That today he meets in groups to not only gather wisdom as to his art, but to voice the basic social principles which imbue and motivate his writing, is logical and possibly a second medium or force by which, in the future, he will express himself and his art, and at the same time advance both—and society. I hope so.

February 1941
(A quotation from Dreiser used as a lead-in to a *Direction* editorial.)

In 1917 and 1918, 123,000 young Americans died for democracy. For democracy another 190,000 were wrecked and maimed physically. Nobody has bothered to count how many more were mentally wrecked for democracy. We know how much democracy has resulted from this human sacrifice. How many of us today, after that lesson, and the lesson of the two decades following, have any clear understanding of the word which we speak and hear more than any other except swell and nuts?

July 1944
"To the People of Europe" (Radio Broadcast, May 1944)

I have just come across the country . . . this great America of ours . . . and I wish you could have been with me. You would have seen, as I did, in railway stations, on trains, in hotels, on the streets . . . an amazing display of youthful vigor, enthusiasm, youthful, yet manly love of country. . . . In sum, millions of the finest type of fighting men, who seek nothing so much as the day and hour when they can try their young strength, their American vitality and brains, their American alertness and inventiveness, against the Nazi brutes, whom they do not fear but whom they abhor, as do all Americans. For what we now know of Nazi principles and practices has inflamed us with the desire to eradicate those principles as well as the criminals who practice them.

If you could cross America with me you would see scores of training fields. Endless divisions that are fair-sized armies . . . marching and drilling in the immense camps in every state of the union. The great wagon-trains with their military equipment. The enormous factories and yards in which everything from ships to airplanes, submarines to tanks, rifles to long-range, heavy artillery are made. Indeed, enormous factories which are minor cities in themselves, from which are pouring out not only ammunition and bombs, but clothing, preserving foods, surgical and medical supplies . . . tents, jeeps, field hospitals and so forth. In fact, I have seen a long, almost endless train go by, stop, and begin to unload cars, trucks, equipment of all kinds . . . until, in a few hours . . . a whole tent city spread out as far as I could see. Presently, men were being called to a meal, over loud-speakers, installed throughout the camp. This tent city, I thought as I saw it, is a demonstration of what our men will soon be setting up in Europe.

There is another side of America's war spirit that I should show you in connection with every military center I visited. You would see new and great armies of women soldiers and nurses, mentally and physically equipped to follow their fighting men not only through the jungles, but, if necessary, to the graves which they may be destined to occupy.

Last but not least, you would and should see the armies of civilians, in every occupation, in every walk of life, who have geared themselves to war . . . and now to invasion . . . who are working for it, hoping for it, ready for it. Retired business men, housewives who have given up their comforts to work in factories. Young girls who work in hospitals to relieve nurses for war duty. Boys who work after school hours, in shops and on farms, to release men for service.

In millions of little homes across America, as I am talking to you now, are farmers coming in from their fields. War workers coming home from factories. Almost the first thing they do is to turn on their radios and listen, as you are listening. They are waiting for news of the invasion, as you are. They are thinking of their boys . . . of the jobs they have to do . . . the fighting, the dying, the killing of the Nazi hordes, as they land and advance into your countries, one by one. They know the price that they, these American fathers and mothers, will have to pay, in lost sons and husbands, in hours of harder work and sacrifices at home.

I personally have been a witness to particular scenes of farewell and departure that have touched me as though the parents and their boys were of my own flesh and blood. A mother, for instance, who, at the moment of parting, turned and ran back . . . only to turn again . . . her eyes wet, and saying . . . "but I mustn't cry, darling, and I won't anymore, but I'll be loving you all the time. My heart is going with you." And again, a crippled father, watching the family car moving away from the door—his son and his bags, and a sister within—hobbling down to the gate, and from there to the nearest corner in the hope of obtaining one lost [*sic*] glimpse of his sturdy son and heir. This boy is overseas now, awaiting the hour of invasion. His family is one of the millions that have but one desire . . . and that is . . . NOW to get the job done . . . by any and every means in their power. To fight at home, to speed invasion, and to crush the Nazi horror forever.

For America glows with the force and enthusiasm of a great and war-ready people, who are determined that Hitler and his criminals shall unconditionally sue for peace. . . . Americans are a great people, a gay people, a fearless people. Cracking jokes, and at the same time making sure that, to the last millionth of an inch, the equipment they prepare is true and fateful, spelling death to our enemies. America is the one country that can say . . . WAIT AND SEE.

Appendix C

Tjader's Contribution to *Direction* Magazine

September-October 1938
"World Youth Congress: Held Last Month in Poughkeepsie, New York."

The beautiful campus of Vassar is teeming with life, gay voices, boys and girls, bare-headed, bare-legged, sunburned, going to where some group deliberates the subject that interests them most, or gathering in lively discussion under the trees. Some lie on the grass, reading, talking, foursomes, twosomes, every race and color, all young (twenty-five is the age limit) and all animated. One cannot help thinking that a new international attitude and mingling of races will make the life, the mating of the future more interesting.

In the main office, young girls come in to type reports, translations—seven or eight of them at one time, typing in as many languages, a furious international click, click, click, not of machine guns, but of instruments of communication, clarification.

In the halls different groups have hung their photographs. Here are Chinese pictures, French Youth Hostels, Our Federal Theater stages, Spanish posters, charts displayed prominently that warn of the danger of syphilis.

"Three-fourths of victims get this disease between the ages of 16-25"—picture of a beautiful girl blind-folded—"one out of every ten get syphilis." The fight is on. Youth is not afraid to fight for its future, unashamed of facts.

And what are the facts that they face today? They have come here to examine them and see what they can do by getting together, by exchanging opinions, by planning action. They have come representing 52 nations, and hundreds of youth groups in these nations, ranging from Catholic Youth to Young Communists. All nations were invited to send representatives. Only Germany and Italy refused the invitation. No Catholic groups came from Canada, Czechoslovakia and other countries. Japan sent a delegate, who declared he would explain and justify his country's invasion of China, but he was not heard from again.

Much could be said, and much has been written about the idealist aims, the fine spirit of these young people. But the purpose of this report is to bring out what they have actually accomplished and to note certain facts which emerge from the special sessions of the Congress.

Four commissions met separately for the first days of the Congress to study political, economic, religious and international problems. On the last days, all met together to coordinate information gathered and vote on resolutions worked out during the Congress. For the purposes of *Direction,* we will examine only the work of the Economic and Cultural Commission.

Education was discussed by delegates of every country, from South America, where almost 40 percent of the population are illiterate, to the big industrial countries, where children are hustled out of schools at the age of fourteen and thrown on the labor market. According to reports from all countries, education is seriously hampered by bad living conditions, undernourishment, poor health supervision, in school and out. These young men and women did not come, hand picked, from a few universities or society clubs. They are the rank and file of the people. And here an unexpected fact emerged. There can be no consideration of education without consideration of the problem of the WORKER which affects the greater part of the people. Then, and then only, can pressure be brought to bear on Governments to better conditions of education, and this will never be done by submitting reports, as some delegates seem to hope, but through Labor Organizations.

This was the remark of an American delegate, who pointed out that it was the first unions in this country which had brought about public schools, which were once considered radical innovations by certain groups who thought the workers should be able to educate their children by private initiative. This led to the question of continued education in training schools or apprenticeship. In many big industries, young people are hired at a rate of two or three dollars a week, as apprentices, at some skilled work.

There are no "junior" labor laws that regulate this period of apprenticeship. Often, young people may work for years, without additional wages, even when they have acquired the skill of trained workers. They consequently keep down the wages of regular workers. In most cases of exploited labor in a trade or factory, workers are found to be largely under twenty-five years of age. Often, young men, discouraged by the long duration of apprenticeship, give up, to take more money as unskilled workers. So they spoil their own chances for getting on in life, and flood the market with unskilled labor. This is particularly true in Belgium and England, where there is no free education after 14 years of age. Here again, education becomes a problem of labor. The real hope of Youth for a square deal is cooperation with the trade unions which could regulate apprenticeship and encourage the extension of free education and training schools up to 16 or 18 years of age. Youth was strongly urged to organize into youth groups and unions as the only way to protect its future. A labor commission for each national Youth Congress was suggested, such as that already in operation here, which should study labor problems and keep in touch with similar commissions in each country, so strengthening the demands of youth in different lands. Amazing facts came out from all countries which showed that except for France and Russia, all countries had virtually the same labor conditions, differing only in degree of want and exploitation. In every case, the disease threatening youth was the same; low wages and bad living conditions.

A girl got up and said she did not see what unionism had to do with Youth. No one knew whether to take her seriously or not. There was a pause, and the discussion went on. Another American delegate cited the case of Western Union employees, 27,000 of whom are around 18 years of age. They are not protected by the Wage and Hour bill and earn on an average of $7.00 per week. The American Congress is helping them to organize.

After a spirited session, an international charter of Youth was proposed, to establish:

A minimum wage
equal pay for equal work

40-hour week
paid vacations
medical supervision and care
organization of Youth into unions

This international charter will form the basis for national charters to be worked out by youth groups in different countries. England and Belgium have already organized "charter" weeks, in which they will formulate their charters after they return from this Congress.

A French delegate pointed out the improvements that have been made for Youth as result of [*sic*] the new Social Laws in France. The chief problem for Youth in France is now the organization of the new leisure into profitable hours of cultural education and sport.

International Students demand cheaper university education.

It is resolved that the Congress endorse the cooperative movement because it builds democracy, helps youth.

Resolved that help should be given to young couples wishing to start a home (wild applause by the youthful delegates!)

A delegate from the Fur Workers Union pointed out that labor has most at stake in the question of Peace. It is only a nation who has nothing to gain from peace that seeks war. Good economic conditions for the worker are the chief guarantee of peace. A healthy and hopeful youth is not fooled by stories of conquest and the glories of war.

At a stirring evening session James J. McDonald, recently returned from the Conference for Refugees in Evian, stated the case for welcoming political exiles:

"Go back and tell your governments that these refugees are potential assets. They have brains and talents sharpened by their experiences. Be intelligently selfish. Some of the finest people in the world are waiting to come to you, the pick of the countries from which they are turning, capable of building a finer civilization elsewhere."

Conclusion

Two important facts emerge from this Congress:

1. The problem of youth and the problem of labor are inseparable.

2. Youth is fearless in its determination to make a brighter future for itself. It will not be enslaved by Fascism because it is well aware that it has

little to gain and everything to lose from giving up its own voice under dictatorship.

It no longer trusts its elders. It throws off the skin of the Old System that no longer works. It is not afraid to try to build a New System. It has already begun its work. As the delegate from the Argentine eloquently declared: "Action is the only creator!"

MODERN AMERICAN LITERATURE
New Approaches

Yoshinobu Hakutani, General Editor

The books in this series deal with many of the major writers known as American realists, modernists, and post-modernists from 1880 to the present. This category of writers will also include less known ethnic and minority writers, a majority of whom are African American, some are Native American, Mexican American, Japanese American, Chinese American, and others. The series might also include studies on well-known contemporary writers, such as James Dickey, Allen Ginsberg, Gary Snyder, John Barth, John Updike, and Joyce Carol Oates. In general, the series will reflect new critical approaches such as deconstructionism, new historicism, psychoanalytical criticism, gender criticism/feminism, and cultural criticism.

For additional information about this series or for the submission of manuscripts, please contact:

Peter Lang Publishing
Acquisitions Department
516 N. Charles St., 2nd Floor
Baltimore, MD 21201